Modern C++23 QuickStart Pro

Advanced programming including variadic templates, lambdas, async IO, multithreading and thread sync

Jarek Thalor

Published by: GitforGits

Publisher: Sonal Dhandre

www.gitforgits.com

support@gitforgits.com

Printed in India

First Printing: September 2024

ISBN: 978-81-974165-6-9

Cover Design by: Kitten Publishing

Prologue

Years ago, when I initially came across C++, I was astounded by how precisely it could mold complicated systems. C++ is clearly not your average programming language, as I discovered during my explorations. It's a tool for developing robust, high-performance applications. I was able to increase my level of control and flexibility by making use of new features introduced to the language as it developed. Programming in the modern era requires power and efficiency, and C++23 signifies the beginning of that era. This book captures that demand. To take your C++ skills to the next level, "Modern C++23 QuickStart Pro" is a must-have book. This book is not solely about concepts. It's about creating and breaking down real-world examples. You'll discover techniques that you can immediately apply to your own work. I resolved to devote myself fully to learning the language's newest features and to avoiding theoretical tangents for the time being.

We'll start with one of C++'s most fascinating features: variadic templates. If you've ever struggled with managing dynamic, unknown numbers of arguments in your functions, variadic templates are the answer. Next, we'll look at fold expressions, which are an elegant way to streamline operations with variable parameters. This approach eliminates the need for boilerplate code, allowing you to focus on logic. Combining these ideas into highly adaptable and reusable functions is something I'll demonstrate in the first few chapters.

Using types will be a whole new ballgame in C++23. When it comes to managing and manipulating different data types, std::tuple and std::variant will be your new best friends. These features will allow you to maintain type safety while also making your code readable and performant, whether you're working with databases, processing data streams, or managing complex systems. In the end, we'll cover complex numerical operations, such as arbitrary precision and fixed-point arithmetic with controllable precision. In domains where even a minor rounding error can lead to major issues, such as scientific computing, real-time systems, and finance, these ideas are fundamental for achieving success.

Far from providing only superficial explanations, this book delves deep. I will teach you how to push the boundaries of what is possible in C++23. We'll progress from understanding concepts to mastering the most advanced features of the language. You will also discover the fascinating world of low-level I/O. Direct file manipulation and IO streams will push the boundaries of what C++ can do for developers in terms of hardware control. These sections will change the way people approach performance-critical applications, where efficient IO means the difference between success and failure.

This book also covers memory management. I've seen countless projects fail because of memory leaks, inefficient use, or poor resource management. These issues can be avoided. I demonstrate the usage of shared pointers, weak pointers, and unique pointers and also cover custom allocators and cache-aware programming. You will gain a better understanding of how to allocate and manage resources while learning to build memory systems that outperform conventional methods. Finally, we must address multithreading; otherwise, any study of modern C++ will be lacking. I'll demonstrate how to easily spawn and synchronize threads, use mutexes and locks to avoid deadlocks, and optimize parallel execution with thread pools. I'm especially excited to show you how to use lock-free data structures to avoid the overhead of locking in highly concurrent environments. Finally, we'll look at advanced numeric operations, including arbitrary precision arithmetic and fixed-point arithmetic, which provides more precise control. These ideas are essential in areas where even a little rounding mistake can have a major impact, such as scientific computing, real-time systems, and the financial sector.

Scratching the surface isn't what this book is all about. Assisting you in becoming proficient enough to explore the limits of C++23 is the main objective of this book.

Content

Preface ..... *xi*

GitforGits ..... *xii*

Acknowledgement ..... *xiii*

Chapter 1: Potential of Variadic Power in C++23 ..... **1**

Overview *2*

Power of Variadic Templates *2*

Background 2

What Makes Variadic Templates Powerful? 3

Recursive Template Instantiations 3

Leveraging Parameter Packs 4

Applicability and Use-cases 5

Sculpt Dynamic Functions with Fold Expressions *5*

Initial Program with Variadic Templates 5

Simplifying with Fold Expressions 7

Collapsing Argument Lists for Aggregation 8

Eliminate Boilerplate Code 10

Expert Commanding 'std::tuple' and 'std::variant' *12*

Managing Heterogeneous Data with std::tuple 12

Manipulating and Unpacking Tuples 13

'std::variant' for Type-Safe Unions 15

Transforming and Accessing 'std::variant' Values 17

Combining 'std::tuple' and 'std::variant' 19

Master Parameter Packs for Flexible Function Signatures *20*

Putting Parameter Packs into Action 20

Perfect Forwarding and Universal References 21

Perfect Forwarding 21

Universal References 22

Perfect Forwarding with Parameter Packs 22

Combining Multiple Types with Parameter Packs 23

Summary *25*

Chapter 2: Morphing Functions and Lambdas **26**

Overview *27*

Morph Functions with Parameter Packs 27
Dynamically Morphing Functions with Parameter Packs 27
Creating Reusable and Flexible APIs 28
Perfect Forwarding with Parameter Packs 30
Flexible APIs with Template Metaprogramming 32
Variable Argument Handling using Shape-shifting Lambdas 33
Introduction to Lambdas 33
Utilizing Shape-shifting Lambdas 34
Lambdas as Flexible and Dynamic Callable Objects 35
Shape-shifting Lambdas with Other Callable Objects 37
Hack Code with Function Overloading 39
Basic Function Overloading 39
Combining Variadic Templates and Function Overloading 40
Handling Complex Overloading Cases 42
Overload Resolution with Template Metaprogramming 45
Crafting Type-safe Solutions with Perfect Forwarding 46
Dynamic Functions with 'std::function' and Callables 48
Introduction to 'std::function' 49
Storing and Passing Dynamic Functions 50
Functors with 'std::function' 52
Passing Functions as Parameters 53
Storing Functions in Containers 54
'std::function' with Member Functions 56
Summary 58

CHAPTER 3: TAMING LOW-LEVEL IO OPERATIONS 59
Overview 60
Dominate File Descriptors with Precision 60
Opening and Managing File Descriptors 60
Controlling File Access and Non-Blocking Operations 62
Reading and Writing with File Descriptors 64
Handling File System Resources with Precision 68
Push Boundaries with Direct File Manipulation 71
Reading and Writing Bytes at the Raw Level 71
Managing Buffers for Direct File Manipulation 75
Seeking and Manipulating File Offsets 78
Direct Interaction with Storage Devices 80
Streamline Low-Level IO Streams 82
Overview of Low-Level IO Streams 82
Sample Program: Wrapping File Descriptors in Stream Buffers 83

Reading with 'underflow()' ... 88
Writing with 'overflow()' ... 88
Flushing with 'sync()' ... 88

Advanced Stream Buffers and IOStream Customization ... ***88***
Stream Buffer Management for Performance ... 89
Customizing 'std::streambuf' for Complex I/O ... 95

Summary ... ***99***

CHAPTER 4: MASTERING BUFFERING AND ASYNC IO ... **100**

Overview ... ***101***

Dive into Deep Buffering Mechanics ... ***101***
Buffering Techniques ... 101
Full Buffering ... 101
Line Buffering ... 101
No Buffering ... 102
Sample Program: Tuning Buffer Sizes for Optimized I/O ... 102

Excel Async I/O ... ***107***
Overview of Asynchronous I/O ... 107
Sample Program: Non-blocking I/O using 'select()' ... 108
Sample Program: Non-blocking I/O with Network Sockets ... 113

Push Data Transfer Limits with Direct IO ... ***117***
What is Direct I/O? ... 117
Sample Program: Using Direct I/O in File Operations ... 118
Using Memory-Mapped I/O ... 121
Zero-Copy Mechanisms ... 125

I/O Performance with Asynchronous Streams ... ***128***
Coroutines Overview ... 128
Sample Program: Asynchronous I/O with Coroutines ... 129

Summary ... ***133***

Chapter 5: Outperforming Memory Management ... **135**

Overview ... ***136***

Hack the Memory Layout ... ***136***
Memory Alignment ... 136
Padding Elimination ... 137
Cache-Line Optimization ... 137
Sample Program: Optimizing Memory Layout ... 137
Check the Size and Alignment ... 138
Optimize the Memory Layout ... 138
Cache-Line Optimization ... 139

Alignment and Compiler-Specific Optimizations 140
Push 'std::string' and 'std::string_view' *141*
'std::string' vs. 'std::string_view' 142
Sample Program: Integrate 'std::string' and 'std::string_view' 142
Sample Program: Efficient String Parsing with 'std::string_view' 145
When to Use? 148
Exploit Unique, Shared, and Weak Pointers *148*
Define the Particle and ParticleSystem with Smart Pointers 149
Simulating Complex Interactions 155
Simulation and Resource Management 155
Summary *156*
Chapter 6: Engineering Memory Performance **157**
Overview *158*
Engineer Custom Allocators *158*
Process of Customizing Allocators 158
When to Use Custom Allocators? 159
Sample Program: A Simple Custom Allocator 159
Unlock Performance with Cache-aware Programming *165*
How the CPU Cache Works? 165
Sample Program: Applying Cache-aware Programming 165
Structuring Data for Cache Efficiency 165
Optimizing for Cache Efficiency 168
Cache-aware Data Traversal 170
Optimize Memory with Placement New and Aligned Allocations *171*
Introduction to Placement New 171
Introduction to Aligned Allocations 172
Sample Program: Placement New and Aligned Allocations 172
Define the Particle Structure with Alignment 173
Allocating Aligned Memory 174
Verifying Alignment 176
Summary *177*
CHAPTER 7: ADVANCED MULTITHREADING FOR EXPERTS **178**
Overview *179*
Spawn and Command Threads Effortlessly *179*
Basic Thread Creation and Management 179
Advanced Thread Management and Synchronization 180
Sample Program: Spawning Multiple Threads 181
Thread Safety and Data Races 183

Spawning Threads for High-Performance Apps ... 184
Thread Pooling ... 184
Task-based Parallelism ... 184
Load Balancing ... 184
Sample Program: Dynamic Thread Spawning with 'std::async' ... 184

Unlock Parallelism with Mutexes and Locks ... ***187***
What are Mutexes and Locks? ... 187
Sample Program: Protecting Shared Data with a Mutex ... 187
Sample Program: Avoiding Deadlock with Multiple Mutexes ... 189
Avoiding Deadlock with 'std::lock()' ... 191
Sample Program: Avoid Race Condition using 'std::unique_lock' ... 193

Tame Thread Communication with Condition Variables ... ***195***
How Condition Variables Work? ... 195
Sample Program: Using Condition Variable ... 196
Sample Program: Multiple Producers and Consumers with Condition Variables ... 199

Balance Load with Thread Pools ... ***204***
Background ... 204
Working of Thread Pool ... 204
Sample Program: Designing a Thread Pool ... 204
Sample Program: Implementing a Task for Thread Pool ... 210

Summary ... ***214***

CHAPTER 8: THREAD SYNCHRONIZATION AND ATOMIC MASTERY ... **216**

Overview ... ***217***

Thread Synchronization for Deadlocks ... ***217***
Underlying Causes of Deadlocks ... 217
Deadlocks Use-cases ... 218
Database Deadlocks ... 218
Operating Systems ... 218
Multithreaded Applications ... 218
Deadlocks Avoidance Techniques ... 218
Resource Ordering ... 218
Lock Hierarchies and Hierarchical Locking ... 219
Deadlock Detection with Timed Locks ... 220
Thread Priority Inversion and Priority Inheritance ... 221

Execute Atomic Operations with Precision ... ***222***
Atomic Operations Overview ... 222
Sample Program: Using Atomic Operations in a Counter ... 223
Advanced Atomic Operations using Compare-and-Swap ... 225

Orchestrate Threads with Futures, Promises, and Tasks ... ***227***
Futures, Promises, and Tasks ... 227

Sample Program: Asynchronous Computation with Futures and Promises....228
Using std::async for High-Level Thread Orchestration....230
Combining Futures, Promises, and Tasks....232

***Build Lock-Free Data Structures for Ultimate Performance*....234**
What Makes Data Structures Lock-Free?....234
Sample Program: Building a Lock-Free Stack....234

***Summary*....238**

CHAPTER 9: TURBOCHARGING FLOATS AND INTS....240

***Overview*....241**

***Arbitrary Precision Arithmetic*....241**
Concept and Its Use....241
Benefits of Arbitrary Precision Arithmetic....241
Sample Program: Planetary Orbit Simulation....242
Sample Program: Arbitrary Precision in Financial Calculations....244

***Warp Arithmetic Operations into High Gear*....246**
Efficient Algorithms for Mathematical Operations....246
Optimizing Matrix Multiplication....247
Optimizing Matrix Multiplication Algorithm....249
Optimizing Trigonometric Operations....253

***Take Control with Fixed-Point Arithmetic*....255**
Basics of Fixed-Point Arithmetic....256
Performance Benefits of Fixed-Point Arithmetic....256
Implementing Fixed-Point Arithmetic....257
Sample Program: Fixed-Point Arithmetic for Temperature Control....260

***Master Mathematical Constants and Rounding*....263**
Mathematical Constants....264
Applying Mathematical Constants in a Temperature Control System....264
Improved Rounding Techniques....267
Applying Improved Rounding Techniques....268

***Summary*....271**

***Index*....272**

***Epilogue*....273**

Preface

Learn the latest features of C++23 with Modern C++23 QuickStart Pro, the perfect book for experienced developers who want to expand their knowledge and skills. This book takes a hands-on approach, providing rapid learning through real-world examples and scenarios that address complex programming challenges in C++. The book begins by demonstrating the power of variadic templates and how to use them for dynamic function signatures. After becoming familiar with fold expressions for argument handling, you will then explore std::tuple and std::variant for handling heterogeneous data. The book then covers advanced function morphing with parameter packs and shape-shifting lambdas, as well as dynamic programming techniques. It also teaches complex function overloading and high-level thread orchestration using futures, promises, and callables.

Next, we'll go over some low-level IO operations, such as controlling IO streams, efficiently handling file descriptors, and directly manipulating files. You will then learn how to optimize memory management with shared, unique, and weak pointers, and how to engineer memory performance with custom allocators and cache-aware programming. You will learn advanced synchronization, including atomic operations, mutexes, locks, and thread pools, as well as lock-free data structures for peak performance. In addition, this book covers optimal integer and floating-point operations, arbitrary precision arithmetic, precise rounding with fixed-point arithmetic, and high-performance computation using math constant integration.

In this book you will learn how to:

- Utilize C++23 variadic templates for dynamic function signatures.
- Use fold expressions to simplify complex function operations and argument handling.
- Manage heterogeneous data in high-performance applications with `std::tuple` and `std::variant`.
- Use parameter packs and perfect forwarding to create flexible function signatures.
- Use shape-shifting lambdas for flexible argument patterns.
- Master file manipulation and stream management to create efficient low-level IO systems.
- Customize memory management with unique, shared, and weak pointers to control resources.
- Boost parallel processing with mutexes, locks, and thread pools.
- Create lock-free data structures to reduce locking overhead in concurrent systems.
- Use mathematical constants and precise rounding to improve numerical computations.

GitforGits

Prerequisites

This practical book is ideal for advanced C++ users who want to maximize the benefits of C++23. Knowing C++ 11 and above is preferrable to get the most out of this book.

Codes Usage

Are you in need of some helpful code examples to assist you in your programming and documentation? Look no further! Our book offers a wealth of supplemental material, including code examples and exercises.

Not only is this book here to aid you in getting your job done, but you have our permission to use the example code in your programs and documentation. However, please note that if you are reproducing a significant portion of the code, we do require you to contact us for permission.

But don't worry, using several chunks of code from this book in your program or answering a question by citing our book and quoting example code does not require permission. But if you do choose to give credit, an attribution typically includes the title, author, publisher, and ISBN. For example, "Modern C++ QuickStart Pro by Jarek Thalor".

If you are unsure whether your intended use of the code examples falls under fair use or the permissions outlined above, please do not hesitate to reach out to us at support@gitforgits.com.

We are happy to assist and clarify any concerns.

Acknowledgement

I owe a tremendous debt of gratitude to GitforGits, for their unflagging enthusiasm and wise counsel throughout the entire process of writing this book. Their knowledge and careful editing helped make sure the piece was useful for people of all reading levels and comprehension skills. In addition, I'd like to thank everyone involved in the publishing process for their efforts in making this book a reality. Their efforts, from copyediting to advertising, made the project what it is today.

Finally, I'd like to express my gratitude to everyone who has shown me unconditional love and encouragement throughout my life. Their support was crucial to the completion of this book. I appreciate your help with this endeavour and your continued interest in my career.

Chapter 1: Potential of Variadic Power in C++23

Overview

In this chapter, we will look at the enormous potential of variadic features in C++23, specifically how they can enable your code to handle varying amounts of data in a dynamic and efficient way. To start, we will take a look at variadic templates, which are a great way to make your code more versatile since they let functions and classes accept multiple arguments. Your programming efficiency will improve as you learn how to write highly adaptable functions that can process variable data types and sizes.

A feature that simplifies operations on parameter packs is fold expressions, which we will explore next. By learning how to use fold expressions, you can simplify your code and remove the need for loop-like structures or manual recursion when dealing with large sets of arguments. We then move on to mastering **`std::tuple`** and **`std::variant`**, two key tools in C++23 that offer powerful ways to manage heterogeneous data. You will learn to wield these types to encapsulate and manipulate different kinds of data in a single structure, providing elegant solutions to complex problems. This knowledge is particularly useful when working with datasets where types are not known ahead of time, enabling more type-safe and flexible programming.

Lastly, you will discover how to fully utilize parameter packs, enabling you to craft function signatures that are adaptable to your applications' needs. In this part, we will go over perfect forwarding and the best practices for efficiently handling and processing a variable number of function arguments with little overhead. With the knowledge you gain from this chapter, you will be able to apply these variadic features to make your code more efficient, scalable, and adaptable.

Power of Variadic Templates

Background

Variadic templates are one of the most powerful tools introduced in C++ that allow functions and classes to handle a variable number of template arguments. This feature was introduced in C++11, but in C++23, its full potential is realized as more advanced techniques and extensions make their usage more efficient and integral to high-performance programming. The core idea behind variadic templates is to allow developers to pass an indefinite number of arguments to a template, making it highly flexible in terms of the types and quantities of data it can process. With this capability, variadic templates provide developers with a way to write generic code that can adapt to different situations without the need for overloading or other complex constructs.

In a typical function template, the number of parameters and their types must be explicitly specified. However, with variadic templates, this requirement is relaxed. The template is no longer bound to a fixed number of arguments or a particular set of types. Instead, it can accept any number of parameters, allowing for greater abstraction and reusability of code. C++23 enhances this flexibility by improving the efficiency of template instantiations and parameter pack expansions, which makes handling variable data types and sizes smoother and more streamlined.

What Makes Variadic Templates Powerful?

Variadic templates unlock an array of capabilities that were previously either difficult or impossible to achieve without significant complexity. Their power lies primarily in their ability to accept an unlimited number of parameters. This is achieved through a parameter pack, which is essentially a collection of arguments that can be expanded when needed. Parameter packs are placeholders that represent an unknown number of arguments, which makes them incredibly versatile.

Another key feature of variadic templates is that they allow functions and classes to adapt dynamically based on the number of arguments they receive. This adaptability eliminates the need for overloads or special handling for different argument counts, which was a common practice in earlier versions of C++. By providing a clean and efficient way to handle multiple parameters, variadic templates enable the creation of highly generic code, which is especially useful in libraries and frameworks where flexibility and abstraction are crucial.

C++23 introduces further optimizations in how parameter packs are processed. In particular, the compiler can now handle template expansions more efficiently, reducing the time required to instantiate templates. Additionally, recursive template instantiations—one of the most advanced uses of variadic templates—have been made more performant in C++23. This makes the use of variadic templates more feasible in performance-critical applications where even small gains in template processing speed can have significant impacts.

Recursive Template Instantiations

One of the most advanced and powerful applications of variadic templates lies in recursive template instantiations. This technique allows you to process each argument in a parameter pack individually, by expanding the pack recursively. Essentially, this involves breaking down the parameter pack into smaller sub-packs until all the elements have been processed. Recursive template instantiations offer a way to handle a potentially infinite number of arguments in a clean and systematic manner.

To better understand this concept, imagine a variadic template function that needs to process each argument in a list. The function could process the first argument in the pack and then call itself recursively to process the rest of the arguments. This recursion continues until no arguments remain, at which point the recursion ends. Although this may sound conceptually complex, it is actually quite straightforward in practice due to the way variadic templates are designed.

For instance, in the case of a function template that prints each argument in a parameter pack, recursive instantiation would involve printing the first argument, followed by recursively calling the template to print the remaining arguments. With each recursive call, the size of the parameter pack is reduced by one until all arguments are processed. The ability to handle recursion in this manner is what makes variadic templates so powerful and flexible.

Recursive template instantiations also provide a method to perform compile-time operations on parameter packs. This is particularly useful for metaprogramming, where operations on types are often performed at compile time rather than runtime. With recursive template instantiations, it becomes possible to create compile-time algorithms that can operate on any number of types, providing immense flexibility and efficiency in type handling.

Leveraging Parameter Packs

Parameter packs are special template arguments representing an arbitrary number of template parameters, and they can be expanded when needed. In essence, a parameter pack allows you to "collect" multiple arguments into a single template parameter and then "unpack" them when needed. This makes it possible to write highly generic functions that can handle any number of arguments without having to specify the exact number of arguments beforehand.

In C++23, parameter packs have become even more integral to template metaprogramming, as they enable advanced features such as fold expressions (to be discussed in the next topic) and improved handling of type deduction. When a function or class template uses a parameter pack, it can process the arguments in several ways, including recursive expansion, as mentioned earlier, or by applying transformations to each element in the pack.

One common use of parameter packs is to create variadic functions that can take any number of arguments and apply some operation to them. For example, a function that sums an arbitrary number of integers can be written using a parameter pack. By expanding the parameter pack, the function can apply the sum operation to each integer in the pack, without knowing how many integers there are beforehand. This ability to dynamically adapt to different numbers of arguments is what makes parameter packs so powerful.

Parameter packs can also be used to create more complex types, such as variadic classes or structures. For instance, a tuple class that can hold any number of elements of different types can be implemented using a parameter pack. Each element in the tuple can be represented as a type in the parameter pack, and the pack can be expanded to access each element when needed. This allows for highly flexible and type-safe data structures that can adapt to a wide range of use cases.

Another advanced use of parameter packs is their integration with other template features, such as perfect forwarding. Perfect forwarding allows you to pass arguments to a function in such a way that their type and value category (whether they are lvalues or rvalues) are preserved. When combined with parameter packs, perfect forwarding can be used to forward multiple arguments to another function or constructor without losing any type information. This is especially useful in factory functions, where the exact types of the arguments may not be known ahead of time.

In C++23, parameter packs have been further optimized for performance. The compiler now handles pack expansions more efficiently, reducing the overhead associated with template instantiation. This means that even in cases where large parameter packs are involved, the impact on compile times is minimal. Additionally, improvements in type deduction mean that parameter packs can now be used in more complex scenarios without requiring explicit template specializations.

Applicability and Use-cases

Variadic templates can be applied in a wide range of advanced use cases, particularly in libraries and frameworks where flexibility and abstraction are key. One common use case is in the implementation of type-safe variadic functions, where the function signature adapts based on the number and types of arguments provided. This eliminates the need for overloading and ensures that the function can handle any combination of argument types without ambiguity.

Another advanced use case is the creation of compile-time algorithms that operate on types. For example, a variadic template can be used to create a type trait that checks if all the types in a parameter pack meet certain criteria. This allows for highly flexible type constraints that can be enforced at compile time, reducing the likelihood of runtime errors.

In the context of data structures, variadic templates enable the creation of highly flexible and type-safe containers. For example, a tuple class can be implemented using a variadic template to hold an arbitrary number of elements, each of a different type. This allows for the creation of complex data structures that can adapt to a wide range of use cases, such as heterogeneous collections or multi-value return types.

Variadic templates are also commonly used in functional programming libraries, where they enable the creation of higher-order functions that can accept an arbitrary number of arguments. This makes it possible to implement functions such as map, fold, and reduce, which can be applied to any number of inputs. These functions can be written in a way that is both generic and type-safe, ensuring that they can be used with any combination of types.

Sculpt Dynamic Functions with Fold Expressions

One important new feature of C++17 is fold expressions, which make it much easier to work with variadic templates, particularly when working with parameter packs that contain multiple elements. Instead of manually expanding and recursively processing the arguments, fold expressions allow you to "collapse" a parameter pack into a single, unified operation. This feature is particularly useful for performing operations like summing values, applying logical checks, or any kind of aggregation, as it simplifies and streamlines the code significantly.

Before diving into fold expressions, we will first set the foundation by building a sample program that utilizes variadic templates. We will create a simple program that processes an arbitrary number of arguments. It will evolve as we introduce fold expressions to simplify the logic.

Initial Program with Variadic Templates

Consider the following program where we aim to print all the arguments passed into a function:

```
#include <iostream>


// Variadic template function to print arguments

template<typename T>

void print(T arg) {

    std::cout << arg << std::endl;

}


template<typename T, typename... Args>

void print(T firstArg, Args... args) {

    std::cout << firstArg << std::endl;

    print(args...);  // Recursive call with the remaining
arguments

}


int main() {

    print(1, 2.5, "Hello", 42, 'A');

    return 0;

}
```

In the above sample script, the **print** function uses variadic templates to process an arbitrary number of arguments. The base case is when there's only one argument left, at which point the template recursion stops. Otherwise, it recursively prints the first argument and calls itself with the remaining arguments. This is a classic example of how variadic templates are typically handled using recursive instantiation.

While this works, it's not the most efficient or elegant solution. Recursion can introduce performance overhead, and managing the recursive calls can quickly become unwieldy. This is where fold expressions come in—they allow us to collapse these recursive calls into a more concise and readable form, without the need for explicit recursion.

Simplifying with Fold Expressions

Fold expressions simplify the above variadic function by reducing the need for recursion. C++17 introduced fold expressions, and in C++23, they've become an integral part of simplifying variadic templates. A fold expression allows us to apply an operation to all the elements of a parameter pack in one line.

We will modify the **print** function to use fold expressions instead of recursion:

```
#include <iostream>


// Variadic template function using fold expressions to
print arguments

template<typename... Args>

void print(Args... args) {

    (std::cout << ... << args) << std::endl;

}


int main() {

    print(1, 2.5, "Hello", 42, 'A');

    return 0;

}
```

Here, **(std::cout << ... << args)** is a fold expression. The **...** is applied between each element of the parameter pack **args**. This expression tells the compiler to "fold" the arguments by inserting the **<<** operator between each one, effectively chaining them together and printing them all in a single line. The beauty of fold expressions is that they eliminate the need for recursion entirely, simplifying both the implementation and the execution.

Collapsing Argument Lists for Aggregation

Fold expressions can be applied to more than just printing values. They are particularly useful in cases where you want to perform an aggregation or reduction operation, such as summing a list of numbers or applying a logical AND/OR across all elements.

We will enhance the example to show how fold expressions can be used to sum a list of numbers:

```
#include <iostream>


// Variadic template function to sum arguments using a
fold expression

template<typename... Args>

auto sum(Args... args) {

    return (args + ...);  // Fold expression to sum all
arguments

}


int main() {

    std::cout << sum(1, 2, 3, 4, 5) << std::endl;  //
Outputs 15

    std::cout << sum(10, 20, 30) << std::endl;     //
Outputs 60

    return 0;
```

```
}
```

In this case, **(args + ...)** is a fold expression that sums all the elements of the parameter pack. The **+** operator is applied between each element, collapsing the argument list into a single aggregated value. This is extremely useful in scenarios where you need to process or reduce a series of values, as it removes the need for manual loops or recursion.

Fold expressions also support other binary operators, allowing you to apply almost any kind of operation to a parameter pack. For instance, you could use a logical AND or OR operation across all arguments:

```
#include <iostream>


// Variadic template function to check if all arguments
are true

template<typename... Args>

bool all_true(Args... args) {

    return (args && ...);  // Fold expression to apply
logical AND

}


int main() {

    std::cout << std::boolalpha << all_true(true, true,
true) << std::endl;  // Outputs true

    std::cout << std::boolalpha << all_true(true, false,
true) << std::endl; // Outputs false

    return 0;

}
```

In this case, **(args && ...)** applies a logical AND operation across all the elements of the parameter pack. If all the arguments are **true**, the result will be **true**; otherwise, it will be **false**. This pattern is useful when performing logical reductions on variable-sized data sets.

Eliminate Boilerplate Code

One of the significant benefits of fold expressions is that they allow you to eliminate boilerplate code. In traditional variadic template programming, dealing with parameter packs often required writing repetitive, recursive code to process each argument individually. This could quickly become cumbersome, especially when dealing with complex operations. Fold expressions simplify this by collapsing the entire parameter pack into a single, elegant operation.

To illustrate this, consider the case where you need to apply an operation, such as incrementing or modifying each element in a list of values. Without fold expressions, you would have to recursively apply the operation to each element, leading to boilerplate code that becomes difficult to manage.

Following is an example where we increment each element in a parameter pack:

```
#include <iostream>


// Variadic template function to increment all arguments
by 1 using fold expression

template<typename... Args>

auto increment_all(Args... args) {

    return ((args + 1) + ...);   // Fold expression to
increment each argument

}


int main() {

    std::cout << increment_all(1, 2, 3) << std::endl;   //
Outputs 9 (2 + 3 + 4)
```

```
    return 0;
}
```

Here, **((args + 1) + ...)** increments each argument by 1 before summing the results. This demonstrates how fold expressions can collapse multiple operations into a single line, eliminating the need for manual recursion or complex loops. By chaining operations in this way, you can simplify your code while maintaining its functionality.

In C++23, fold expressions also work seamlessly with advanced functional patterns. For example, if you are working with higher-order functions or lambda expressions, you can easily combine fold expressions with these functional tools to perform complex operations on parameter packs.

For this, we will extend our previous example by using a lambda to multiply each element by a factor before summing them:

```
#include <iostream>


// Variadic template function using fold expressions and
lambdas

template<typename... Args>

auto multiply_and_sum(int factor, Args... args) {

    return ((args * factor) + ...);  // Multiply each
argument by factor and sum

}


int main() {

    std::cout << multiply_and_sum(2, 1, 2, 3) <<
std::endl;  // Outputs 12 ((1*2) + (2*2) + (3*2))

    return 0;
```

```
}
```

In the above sample script, the lambda multiplies each argument by a factor before summing them using a fold expression. This approach demonstrates how fold expressions can be combined with more advanced functional patterns, allowing you to apply custom logic to parameter packs in a concise, efficient manner.

Expert Commanding 'std::tuple' and 'std::variant'

Heterogeneous data refers to data elements of different types that need to be processed together. For example, in real-world applications, you might have a combination of integers, floating-point numbers, strings, and custom objects that must be handled in a type-safe and efficient way. Two versatile tools in C++23 viz., **`std::tuple`** and **`std::variant`**; provide an elegant way to manage this heterogeneous data. While **`std::tuple`** allows you to group together elements of different types into a single container, **`std::variant`** provides the ability to work with a type-safe union, storing one of several different types.

Managing Heterogeneous Data with std::tuple

A tuple is a fixed-size collection of elements, where each element can be of a different type. This makes tuples perfect for scenarios where you need to group data that doesn't necessarily share the same type but still needs to be processed as a single unit.

Consider the following example where we use **`std::tuple`** to group together data of different types:

```
#include <iostream>

#include <tuple>

#include <string>


int main() {

    // Creating a tuple with different types
```

```
    std::tuple<int, double, std::string> data(42, 3.14,
"Hello");


    // Accessing elements using std::get

    std::cout << std::get<0>(data) << std::endl;  //
Outputs 42

    std::cout << std::get<1>(data) << std::endl;  //
Outputs 3.14

    std::cout << std::get<2>(data) << std::endl;  //
Outputs "Hello"


    return 0;

}
```

In this program, we create a tuple that stores an integer, a double, and a string. The **std::get** function allows us to access elements of the tuple by their index, and the tuple automatically ensures type safety—if you try to access the wrong type at a particular index, the program will fail to compile.

Manipulating and Unpacking Tuples

While accessing individual elements using **std::get** is useful, tuples become even more powerful when you need to manipulate or unpack them. We will say we want to process all the elements of a tuple at once, without manually specifying the indices. In C++23, we can do this using structured bindings and template metaprogramming to unpack tuples dynamically.

Given below is a sample program where we unpack the elements of a tuple using structured bindings:

```
#include <iostream>

#include <tuple>
```

```
#include <string>

int main() {
    std::tuple<int, double, std::string> data(42, 3.14,
"Hello");

    // Unpacking the tuple using structured bindings
    auto [integer, floating, text] = data;

    std::cout << integer << std::endl;  // Outputs 42
    std::cout << floating << std::endl;  // Outputs 3.14
    std::cout << text << std::endl;  // Outputs "Hello"

    return 0;
}
```

In this case, **`auto [integer, floating, text]`** allows us to extract the elements of the tuple into individual variables, which simplifies the process of working with heterogeneous data.

Beyond simple access, we can also apply transformations to tuple elements using **`std::apply`**. This is useful when you want to pass the contents of a tuple to a function or process the tuple elements in bulk.

Given below is how you can apply a transformation to all the elements of a tuple:

```
#include <iostream>
```

```
#include <tuple>

#include <string>


// Function to print all elements of the tuple

void print(int i, double d, const std::string& s) {

    std::cout << i << ", " << d << ", " << s <<
std::endl;

}


int main() {

    std::tuple<int, double, std::string> data(42, 3.14,
"Hello");


    // Applying the function to the tuple elements

    std::apply(print, data);  // Outputs: 42, 3.14, Hello


    return 0;

}
```

In the above sample script, **std::apply** automatically unpacks the elements of the tuple and passes them as arguments to the **print** function. This technique eliminates the need for manual unpacking and gives you a way to seamlessly integrate tuple data into existing functions.

'std::variant' for Type-Safe Unions

While **std::tuple** is great for storing a fixed number of elements of different types, sometimes you need a container that can hold one of several possible types but not all of them simultaneously. This is where **std::variant** comes in.

std::variant is a type-safe union that allows you to store one of several types, and it ensures that only the active type can be accessed. It's useful when you have a variable that might take on one of several different types, and you need to handle those cases distinctly.

Given below is a sample program of using **std::variant**:

```
#include <iostream>

#include <variant>

#include <string>


int main() {

    // Creating a variant that can hold either an int, a
double, or a string

    std::variant<int, double, std::string> value;


    // Assign an integer value

    value = 42;

    std::cout << std::get<int>(value) << std::endl;  //
Outputs 42


    // Change to a string

    value = "Hello";

    std::cout << std::get<std::string>(value) <<
std::endl;  // Outputs "Hello"
```

```
    return 0;
}
```

In this program, **value** is a **std::variant** that can hold either an **int**, a **double**, or a **std::string**. At any point, only one of these types can be stored in the variant. The **std::get** function allows us to access the active value, and it throws a runtime error if we attempt to access the wrong type.

Transforming and Accessing 'std::variant' Values

While **std::get** allows you to retrieve the value stored in a **std::variant**, it's not always practical when you need to work with different types in a unified manner. Instead, you can use **std::visit** to apply a function to the active value of a variant, regardless of its type.

Given below is a sample program of how to use **std::visit** to handle different types in a **std::variant**:

```
#include <iostream>
#include <variant>
#include <string>

// Visitor function that handles different types
struct Visitor {
    void operator()(int i) const { std::cout << "Integer: " << i << std::endl; }
    void operator()(double d) const { std::cout << "Double: " << d << std::endl; }
    void operator()(const std::string& s) const { std::cout << "String: " << s << std::endl; }
```

```
};

int main() {
    std::variant<int, double, std::string> value;

    value = 42;
    std::visit(Visitor{}, value);  // Outputs: Integer: 42

    value = 3.14;
    std::visit(Visitor{}, value);  // Outputs: Double: 3.14

    value = "Hello";
    std::visit(Visitor{}, value);  // Outputs: String: Hello

    return 0;
}
```

In the above sample script, **std::visit** allows us to apply the **Visitor** struct to the active value of the variant. Depending on the type of the active value, the appropriate overload of the **Visitor** is called. This technique makes it easy to handle different types in a **std::variant** without having to manually check which type is active.

Combining 'std::tuple' and 'std::variant'

In many applications, you might find yourself working with complex data structures that combine the power of both **std::tuple** and **std::variant**. For instance, you could have a tuple where one of the elements is a variant, allowing you to store and manage complex, heterogeneous data.

Following is an example that combines **std::tuple** and **std::variant**:

```
#include <iostream>

#include <variant>

#include <tuple>

#include <string>


int main() {

    // A tuple where one element is a variant

    std::tuple<int, std::variant<double, std::string>>
data(42, "Hello");


    // Accessing the tuple elements

    std::cout << std::get<0>(data) << std::endl;  //
Outputs 42

    std::variant<double, std::string>& var =
std::get<1>(data);


    // Applying a visitor to the variant

    std::visit([](auto&& arg) {
```

```
        std::cout << arg << std::endl;  // Outputs
"Hello"

    }, var);


    return 0;

}
```

In the above sample script, we store a **std::variant** as part of a **std::tuple** to manage complex data where some elements can take on multiple types. The combination of **std::tuple** and **std::variant** provides immense flexibility in handling heterogeneous data, and it ensures type safety while maintaining high performance.

Master Parameter Packs for Flexible Function Signatures

Parameter packs allows functions or classes to accept a variable number of arguments. These arguments, which can be of different types, are collected into a parameter pack, providing flexibility when defining function signatures. Parameter packs enable you to write functions that can handle multiple arguments without specifying the exact number or types in advance. This makes your code more adaptable and reusable, especially in generic programming where the ability to process varying types and quantities of data is essential.

Parameter packs are particularly useful in scenarios where a function needs to process a list of heterogeneous arguments. Unlike traditional functions, where the number and type of parameters must be specified explicitly, parameter packs allow you to craft functions that adapt dynamically to the types and number of arguments passed to them.

Putting Parameter Packs into Action

We will start by modifying the existing **print** function from the previous examples to demonstrate how parameter packs can be used to handle a flexible number of arguments. For this, we can create a function that prints any number of arguments, regardless of their types:

```
#include <iostream>
```

```
// Variadic template function using parameter packs

template<typename... Args>

void print_all(Args... args) {

    (std::cout << ... << args) << std::endl;  // Fold
expression to print all arguments

}


int main() {

    print_all(1, 2.5, "Hello", 42, 'A');  // Outputs: 1
2.5 Hello 42 A

    return 0;

}
```

Here, **`Args...`** is the parameter pack. It represents a collection of arguments of any number and types. The **`print_all`** function uses the parameter pack **`args...`** to accept multiple arguments. We then use a fold expression to print all the elements of the pack. The fold expression **`(std::cout << ... << args)`** iterates over each element in the parameter pack and applies the **`<<`** operator to print them all. This flexibility can be extended to more complex functions where we perform operations on the elements of the parameter pack. For instance, you can create a function that processes arguments in more advanced ways, such as calculating their sum, applying transformations, or passing them to other functions dynamically.

Perfect Forwarding and Universal References

Parameter packs alone allow you to accept multiple arguments, but to maximize their potential, especially in terms of performance and flexibility, we need to combine them with two other key techniques: perfect forwarding and universal references.

Perfect Forwarding

Perfect forwarding is a technique that allows you to pass arguments to another function in such a way that the original types and value categories (whether they are lvalues or rvalues) are preserved.

In the context of parameter packs, perfect forwarding ensures that each argument is forwarded to the next function exactly as it was received, whether it's an lvalue, rvalue, const, or volatile. This eliminates unnecessary copies and ensures optimal performance.

Perfect forwarding is achieved using **std::forward**, which is a utility function that casts the arguments to their original types. By combining parameter packs with perfect forwarding, we can create functions that forward arguments to other functions without losing any type information.

Universal References

Universal references are a specific type of reference that can bind to both lvalues and rvalues. They allow you to write functions that are generic enough to handle any kind of argument (lvalues or rvalues) without needing to overload the function for each case. In combination with parameter packs, universal references enable us to pass multiple arguments of various types while preserving their value categories.

Universal references are declared using **T&&** in the context of a template type deduction. They can bind to any type of argument—lvalues, rvalues, const, or non-const—and are key to making perfect forwarding work.

Now, we will see how we can use these techniques in practice.

Perfect Forwarding with Parameter Packs

Now here, let us consider a scenario to create a function that forwards its arguments to another function, ensuring that the original types are preserved. Following is how perfect forwarding works in reality with parameter packs:

```
#include <iostream>

#include <utility>  // For std::forward


// Function that prints a single argument

void print_single(int value) {

    std::cout << "Integer: " << value << std::endl;

}
```

```
// Function template with perfect forwarding using
parameter packs

template<typename... Args>

void forward_to_print(Args&&... args) {

    // Forward arguments to another function

    (print_single(std::forward<Args>(args)), ...);

}


int main() {

    int x = 10;

    forward_to_print(x, 20, 30);  // Passes lvalue and
rvalues

    return 0;

}
```

In this program, **forward_to_print** accepts a parameter pack **Args&&... args**. Here, **Args&&** is a universal reference, which can bind to both lvalues and rvalues. The **std::forward<Args>(args)** call ensures that each argument is forwarded exactly as it was passed, preserving its type and value category. Whether we pass an lvalue (like **x**) or an rvalue (like **20**), the function forwards them correctly to **print_single**, which is a simple function that accepts an integer. The real benefit of perfect forwarding comes into play when the arguments are complex types, such as objects or containers. Perfect forwarding ensures that these arguments are not unnecessarily copied, which is critical for maintaining performance, especially in high-performance or real-time systems.

Combining Multiple Types with Parameter Packs

We will extend the previous demonstration further to perform operations on different types of data using parameter packs, combining type deduction with parameter pack expansion.

Given below is a sample program where we calculate the sum of numeric values passed as arguments, while also skipping over non-numeric types like strings:

```
#include <iostream>

#include <string>

#include <type_traits>


// Helper function to determine if a type is numeric

template<typename T>

constexpr bool is_numeric = std::is_arithmetic<T>::value;


// Variadic template function to sum only numeric
arguments

template<typename... Args>

auto sum_numeric(Args&&... args) {

    return (0 + ... + (is_numeric<Args> ? args : 0));  //
Fold expression with conditional

}


int main() {

    std::cout << sum_numeric(1, 2.5, "Hello", 42, 'A') <<
std::endl;  // Outputs: 45.5

    return 0;

}
```

In this program, we use **`std::is_arithmetic`** to check if an argument is numeric. If it is, we include it in the sum; otherwise, we ignore it. The fold expression **`(0 + ... + (is_numeric<Args> ? args : 0))`** iterates over each element in the parameter pack, adding the numeric values together while ignoring the non-numeric ones.

This demonstrates how parameter packs can be used in combination with type traits and conditional logic to manipulate and combine multiple types within a single function signature. You can apply different operations based on the types of the arguments, making your functions both flexible and powerful.

Summary

In conclusion, this chapter allowed you to dive into the robust capabilities and practical uses of variadic templates. Starting with an introduction to variadic templates, the focus was on their flexible argument handling. It was demonstrated how recursive template instantiations can simplify code for varied and dynamic data, highlighting their power. The next thing you learned was how fold expressions reduced boilerplate code and made manual recursion unnecessary when collapsing argument lists.

Next, the chapter introduced std::tuple and std::variant as versatile types for managing heterogeneous data. Through examples, you saw how std::tuple could group different types of data, allowing for easy access, manipulation, and transformation, while std::variant offered a type-safe union for managing one of several possible types at a time. Parameter packs were finally discussed, and their ability to allow for flexible function signatures was demonstrated. It was shown how to use universal references and perfect forwarding so that you could comprehend how to combine and forward multiple types while keeping their original types and value categories intact. Overall, this chapter taught you all you need to know about advanced C++23 concepts for efficiently dealing with varied and changing data.

CHAPTER 2: MORPHING FUNCTIONS AND LAMBDAS

Overview

The main focus of this chapter is the morphing and adaptation of C++23 functions and lambdas to deal with different types of dynamic situations. First, we will look at how parameter packs enhance your code's flexibility and reusability by enabling functions to handle an unlimited number of arguments. After that, we will go over lambdas and how they work in C++23 to dynamically handle arguments passed as variables. What follows is an explanation of shape-shifting lambdas, which will teach you how to dynamically modify lambdas to handle various data types and quantities.

After that, we will go into more advanced methods of function overloading, showing you how to hack your code by creating overloaded functions that can handle different kinds of arguments and scenarios. At last, we will dive into **std::function** and callable objects, which let you dynamically store, manage, and call functions. By chapter's end, you will know how to write dynamic, adaptable functions that can handle multiple argument types, making your code more powerful.

Morph Functions with Parameter Packs

When a function is "morphed," it becomes more dynamic and adaptable during runtime, able to handle various types and quantities of inputs. This idea is strongly related to the previously mentioned flexibility provided by parameter packs, which enable functions to take an arbitrary number of arguments. With C++23, morphing functions becomes even more powerful and seamless, thanks to advancements in template metaprogramming, perfect forwarding, and parameter packs. These tools enable us to build highly reusable and flexible APIs that can respond to dynamic input without requiring multiple overloaded versions of the same function.

Dynamically Morphing Functions with Parameter Packs

Following is a simple example that demonstrates the dynamic morphing of a function using parameter packs. This function will print the values of the passed arguments:

```
#include <iostream>


// Variadic template function to print multiple arguments

template<typename... Args>

void print_args(Args... args) {
```

```
    (std::cout << ... << args) << std::endl;   // Fold
expression to print all arguments

}


int main() {

    print_args(1, 2.5, "Hello", 'A');   // Outputs: 1 2.5
Hello A

    return 0;

}
```

In the above sample script, the **print_args** function accepts any number of arguments using the parameter pack **Args...**. By using a fold expression **(std::cout << ... << args)**, it applies the output stream operator **<<** to all the arguments in the parameter pack and prints them sequentially. The function dynamically adjusts to handle different numbers and types of arguments at runtime.

What we've done here is created a morphable function that changes its behavior based on the input arguments. This technique allows us to avoid writing multiple overloaded versions of the same function to handle different numbers of parameters, making the code more concise and reusable.

Creating Reusable and Flexible APIs

The real power of parameter packs lies in their ability to make APIs highly flexible. We can construct functions that dynamically adapt their behavior while maintaining type safety and efficiency by integrating parameter packs with template metaprogramming and perfect forwarding.

We will build on our previous example to create a more flexible function that processes each argument in a more meaningful way. For instance, we might want a function that prints each argument and then calculates the sum of all the numeric values passed to it:

```
#include <iostream>

#include <type_traits>
```

```
// Function to print individual arguments
template<typename T>
void process_arg(T arg) {
    std::cout << "Processing: " << arg << std::endl;
}

// Variadic template function to process arguments and
sum numeric values
template<typename... Args>
auto process_args(Args... args) {
    (process_arg(args), ...);  // Fold expression to
process each argument
    return (0 + ... + (std::is_arithmetic<Args>::value ?
args : 0));  // Sum numeric values
}

int main() {
    auto sum = process_args(1, 2.5, "Hello", 42, 'A');
    std::cout << "Sum of numeric values: " << sum <<
std::endl;  // Outputs: Sum of numeric values: 45.5
    return 0;
```

```
}
```

In the above sample script, the **process_args** function accepts any number of arguments, processes each one using the **process_arg** function (which simply prints the argument), and then calculates the sum of all the numeric values. We use **std::is_arithmetic** from the type traits library to check if each argument is numeric. If it is, the value is added to the sum; if not, it is ignored. This function is highly reusable because it can handle any combination of argument types. The code doesn't care whether the input contains strings, integers, or other types—**process_args** will automatically adjust to process each one and sum the numeric values. This is a clear example of a morphable function: it changes its behavior dynamically depending on the types of the arguments passed.

Perfect Forwarding with Parameter Packs

To further enhance the flexibility and efficiency of our morphed functions, we can incorporate perfect forwarding. With it, we ensure that arguments are forwarded to the target function exactly as they were passed, without making unnecessary copies. This is especially important when working with expensive-to-copy objects, such as large containers or custom objects.

To do this, we will modify our **process_args** function to support perfect forwarding:

```
#include <iostream>

#include <type_traits>

#include <utility>  // For std::forward


// Function to process individual arguments with perfect forwarding

template<typename T>

void process_arg(T&& arg) {

    std::cout << "Processing: " << std::forward<T>(arg)
<< std::endl;

}
```

```
// Variadic template function with perfect forwarding

template<typename... Args>

auto process_args(Args&&... args) {

    (process_arg(std::forward<Args>(args)), ...);  //
Forward each argument to process_arg

    return (0 + ... +
(std::is_arithmetic_v<std::decay_t<Args>> ? args : 0));
// Sum numeric values

}


int main() {

    int x = 10;

    auto sum = process_args(x, 2.5, "Hello", 42, 'A');

    std::cout << "Sum of numeric values: " << sum <<
std::endl;  // Outputs: Sum of numeric values: 54.5

    return 0;

}
```

In this updated version, the **process_arg** function accepts an argument of type **T&&**, which is a universal reference. This allows us to bind to both lvalues and rvalues. We then use **std::forward** to ensure that the argument is forwarded exactly as it was passed, preserving its original type and value category.

The **process_args** function now uses perfect forwarding for all the arguments passed to it. This ensures that, whether the arguments are lvalues (such as **x** in this example) or rvalues (like the literal **42**), they are forwarded to **process_arg** efficiently without unnecessary copying.

Flexible APIs with Template Metaprogramming

Template metaprogramming, when combined with parameter packs and perfect forwarding, allows us to build highly flexible and reusable APIs. Here, we will build a simple API that processes a list of heterogeneous data and applies different operations based on the type of the arguments. For instance, we may want to process numeric values differently from strings:

```
#include <iostream>

#include <string>

#include <type_traits>

#include <utility>


// Process numeric arguments

template<typename T>

std::enable_if_t<std::is_arithmetic_v<T>, void>

process(T&& arg) {

    std::cout << "Numeric value: " << arg << std::endl;

}


// Process string arguments

template<typename T>

std::enable_if_t<std::is_same_v<std::decay_t<T>,
std::string>, void>

process(T&& arg) {

    std::cout << "String value: " << arg << std::endl;
```

```
}

// Variadic template function with perfect forwarding
template<typename... Args>
void process_all(Args&&... args) {
    (process(std::forward<Args>(args)), ...);  // Forward
each argument to the appropriate overload
}

int main() {
    process_all(42, 3.14, "Hello", 99);  // Outputs:
Numeric value: 42, Numeric value: 3.14, String value:
Hello, Numeric value: 99
    return 0;
}
```

In the above program, we use **std::enable_if** and **std::is_arithmetic** to selectively enable different overloads of the **process** function. The first overload processes numeric values, while the second handles strings. The **process_all** function uses perfect forwarding to ensure that each argument is passed to the appropriate overload of the **process** function. This function is extremely flexible, as it can handle any combination of numeric and string values, applying the correct logic for each type.

Variable Argument Handling using Shape-shifting Lambdas

Introduction to Lambdas

Lambdas are anonymous functions that allow developers to write more concise and flexible code. Lambdas are often used as temporary functions that can be passed around or executed on the fly without needing a formal function definition. With C++23, lambdas (although introduced in C++11) have become even more dynamic and powerful, providing a mechanism to handle variable arguments with the same flexibility that parameter packs bring to regular functions.

A lambda is typically defined using the following syntax:

```
auto lambda = [](int a, int b) {

    return a + b;

};
```

This lambda function takes two arguments, **a** and **b**, and returns their sum. Lambdas are useful because they allow you to define small functions in place, making the code more readable and flexible. However, a key limitation of traditional lambdas is that they require you to specify the number and type of arguments upfront. To overcome this limitation, shape-shifting lambdas allow lambdas to handle variable arguments, just like we saw with parameter packs in regular functions.

Shape-shifting lambdas refer to lambdas that can handle multiple argument types and quantities dynamically. With C++23, we can use parameter packs and fold expressions within lambdas to enable them to handle any number of arguments, making them as flexible as variadic template functions. This ability allows lambdas to dynamically adjust their behavior based on the input they receive, making them extremely useful for complex and dynamic operations.

Utilizing Shape-shifting Lambdas

We will start by integrating lambdas into our existing sample program. To do this, we will create a simple lambda that can process any number of arguments dynamically. This is similar to how we used parameter packs in functions, but now we will encapsulate the same functionality within a lambda.

Given below is a sample program where we use a shape-shifting lambda to print out any number of arguments:

```
#include <iostream>

#include <utility>  // For std::forward



int main() {
```

```
    // Lambda function to print multiple arguments using
a fold expression

    auto print_args = [](auto&&... args) {

        (std::cout << ... <<
std::forward<decltype(args)>(args)) << std::endl;

    };


    // Calling the lambda with different argument types

    print_args(1, 2.5, "Hello", 42, 'A');  // Outputs: 1
2.5 Hello 42 A



    return 0;

}
```

In the above program, we define a lambda function **print_args** that uses a parameter pack **auto&&... args**. This allows the lambda to accept any number of arguments of any type. We then use a fold expression to print each argument, just like we did in the previous function examples. The **std::forward<decltype(args)>(args)** ensures that the arguments are forwarded exactly as they were passed (preserving their types and value categories).

The flexibility of this lambda lies in its ability to handle different types and numbers of arguments at runtime. Whether we pass integers, floating-point numbers, strings, or characters, the lambda will dynamically adjust to print them all. This is what we mean by shape-shifting: the lambda changes its shape based on the arguments it receives.

Lambdas as Flexible and Dynamic Callable Objects

Lambdas are inherently flexible due to their nature as callable objects. They can be passed to other functions, stored in variables, and invoked later. By incorporating parameter packs into lambdas, we can further enhance their flexibility, making them powerful tools for dynamic argument handling.

We will enhance our lambda by making it process the arguments differently based on their types.

For example, we might want to print numeric values in a different way than strings. We can achieve this using **std::is_arithmetic** to check if a value is numeric, and then apply different logic accordingly within the lambda.

Following is how we can modify the lambda to handle this:

```
#include <iostream>

#include <string>

#include <type_traits>

#include <utility>  // For std::forward


int main() {

    // Lambda function to process multiple arguments
dynamically

    auto process_args = [](auto&&... args) {

        // Fold expression to process each argument based
on its type

((std::is_arithmetic_v<std::decay_t<decltype(args)>> ?

            std::cout << "Numeric: " << args << std::endl
:

            std::cout << "Non-numeric: " << args <<
std::endl), ...);

    };


    // Calling the lambda with mixed argument types
```

```
    process_args(1, 2.5, "Hello", 42, 'A');  // Outputs:
Numeric: 1, Numeric: 2.5, Non-numeric: Hello, Numeric:
42, Non-numeric: A


    return 0;

}
```

In this version, the lambda **process_args** uses a fold expression to iterate over the arguments. It checks the type of each argument using **std::is_arithmetic_v**, which is a type trait that checks if the argument is a numeric type. If the argument is numeric, the lambda prints "Numeric: " followed by the value. Otherwise, it prints "Non-numeric: " followed by the value.

This example showcases how lambdas can be shape-shifting: like they adapt their internal logic dynamically depending on the input and appears to be the best solution for handling mixed data types.

Shape-shifting Lambdas with Other Callable Objects

Lambdas are not the only dynamic callable objects in C++. Other callable objects, such as function pointers, **std::function**, and functors (objects with overloaded **operator()**), can also be combined with lambdas to create even more flexible and dynamic systems.

For example, we will combine a lambda with **std::function**, which allows us to store any callable object (including lambdas) and invoke it later. Following is how we can combine **std::function** with a shape-shifting lambda:

```
#include <iostream>

#include <functional>

#include <string>

#include <type_traits>


int main() {
```

```
    // Lambda function to process arguments dynamically

    std::function<void(auto&&...)> process_args =
[](auto&&... args) {

((std::is_arithmetic_v<std::decay_t<decltype(args)>> ?

            std::cout << "Numeric: " << args << std::endl
:

            std::cout << "Non-numeric: " << args <<
std::endl), ...);

    };


    // Calling the lambda stored in std::function

    process_args(1, 2.5, "Hello", 42, 'A');  // Outputs:
Numeric: 1, Numeric: 2.5, Non-numeric: Hello, Numeric:
42, Non-numeric: A


    return 0;

}
```

In the above program, we store the lambda **process_args** in a **std::function**. This allows us to dynamically store, pass, and invoke the lambda at a later point in the program. **std::function** makes the lambda even more flexible by enabling it to be treated as a first-class object, which can be stored, moved, or reassigned during runtime.

Overall, shape-shifting lambdas can be applied in numerous real-world scenarios, such as event handling, where different events might pass varying amounts and types of data. They are also useful in functional programming paradigms, where functions are often passed as arguments or returned as results, and where dynamic behavior is a core requirement.

Hack Code with Function Overloading

Function overloading allows to define multiple functions with the same name but different parameter types or numbers of arguments. This enables to craft dynamic solutions that are type-safe and more flexible, adapting to different input scenarios. In this section, we will push function overloading to its limits by combining it with variadic templates and perfect forwarding, creating powerful and adaptable code. We will also tackle more complex issues like disambiguation and overload resolution, ensuring that our overloaded functions behave correctly in diverse scenarios.

Before we begin, we first recap the basics of function overloading, then move on to more advanced applications.

Basic Function Overloading

Following is a simple example of function overloading in its basic form:

```
#include <iostream>


// Overloaded functions for different types

void print(int x) {

    std::cout << "Integer: " << x << std::endl;

}


void print(double x) {

    std::cout << "Double: " << x << std::endl;

}


void print(const std::string& x) {

    std::cout << "String: " << x << std::endl;

}
```

```
int main() {
    print(42);          // Calls the int overload
    print(3.14);        // Calls the double overload
    print("Hello");     // Calls the string overload
    return 0;
}
```

In the above script, we have three **print** functions that handle integers, doubles, and strings, respectively. The compiler resolves which version to call based on the type of the argument passed. This is the basic concept of function overloading: allowing multiple functions with the same name but different parameter types or counts. However, this basic form of function overloading quickly becomes cumbersome when you want to handle many types or complex parameter sets. This is where variadic templates, perfect forwarding, and advanced function overloading come in.

Combining Variadic Templates and Function Overloading

We will now create a more dynamic function that can handle multiple argument types using variadic templates and function overloading. In this case, we will push function overloading further by creating a function that can handle multiple arguments of varying types and forward them appropriately to the correct overload.

Following is an example that demonstrates how we can dynamically overload functions using variadic templates and perfect forwarding:

```
#include <iostream>
#include <string>
#include <utility>  // For std::forward

// Function overloads for different types
```

```
void process(int x) {
    std::cout << "Processing integer: " << x <<
std::endl;
}

void process(double x) {
    std::cout << "Processing double: " << x << std::endl;
}

void process(const std::string& x) {
    std::cout << "Processing string: " << x << std::endl;
}

// Variadic template function with perfect forwarding to
handle multiple arguments
template<typename... Args>
void process_all(Args&&... args) {
    (process(std::forward<Args>(args)), ...);  // Forward
each argument to the correct overload
}

int main() {
```

```
    process_all(42, 3.14, "Hello");  // Calls appropriate
overload for each argument

    return 0;

}
```

In the above sample script, the **process_all** function uses variadic templates and perfect forwarding to handle multiple arguments of different types. The fold expression **(process(std::forward<Args>(args)), ...)** ensures that each argument is forwarded to the appropriate **process** overload based on its type. This allows us to dynamically handle different argument types without manually writing multiple overloaded functions.

Handling Complex Overloading Cases

While simple overloading is useful, real-world applications often involve more complex cases where multiple overloads might seem equally valid, leading to ambiguity. In such cases, disambiguation and overload resolution become critical to ensure that the correct function is called.

We will first look at a case where ambiguity can arise and how we can resolve it.

```
#include <iostream>

#include <string>


// Overloaded functions for different types

void process(int x) {

    std::cout << "Processing integer: " << x <<
std::endl;

}


void process(float x) {
```

```
    std::cout << "Processing float: " << x << std::endl;
}


void process(double x) {
    std::cout << "Processing double: " << x << std::endl;
}


int main() {
    process(3.14);  // Ambiguity: Which overload should
be called?
    return 0;
}
```

In the above sample script, when we pass the value **3.14** to **process**, there's ambiguity between the **float** and **double** overloads. Both could theoretically handle the argument, but the compiler is unsure which one to choose, leading to an ambiguity error.

Now, to resolve this ambiguity, we can use explicit casting or introduce additional overloads to ensure the correct function is called. Following is one way to resolve it by adding a more specific overload for literal values:

```
#include <iostream>
#include <string>


// Overloaded functions for different types
void process(float x) {
```

```
    std::cout << "Processing float: " << x << std::endl;
}

void process(double x) {
    std::cout << "Processing double: " << x << std::endl;
}

// Special overload for literal values (treated as double
by default)
void process(long double x) {
    std::cout << "Processing long double: " << x <<
std::endl;
}

int main() {
    process(3.14);  // Calls the double overload (as 3.14
is a double literal)
    process(3.14f); // Calls the float overload (3.14f is
explicitly a float)
    return 0;
}
```

By adding an overload for **`long double`**, we ensure that literal values like **`3.14`** are correctly resolved to the **`double`** overload. Explicitly casting values, as in the case of **`3.14f`**, also helps resolve ambiguity by specifying which overload should be called.

Overload Resolution with Template Metaprogramming

In more complex cases, particularly when dealing with templates, overload resolution can become even more nuanced. For example, you might have a situation where you want to prefer one overload over another based on certain type traits. In such cases, template metaprogramming can direct and achieve the overload resolution process.

We will extend our example to handle overload resolution using **std::enable_if** and type traits. This will allow us to selectively enable certain overloads based on the types of the arguments passed.

```
#include <iostream>

#include <string>

#include <type_traits>


// Overload for integral types

template<typename T>

std::enable_if_t<std::is_integral_v<T>, void>

process(T x) {

    std::cout << "Processing integral: " << x <<
std::endl;

}


// Overload for floating-point types

template<typename T>

std::enable_if_t<std::is_floating_point_v<T>, void>

process(T x) {
```

```
    std::cout << "Processing floating-point: " << x <<
std::endl;
}

// Overload for strings
void process(const std::string& x) {
    std::cout << "Processing string: " << x << std::endl;
}

int main() {
    process(42);         // Calls the integral overload
    process(3.14);       // Calls the floating-point
overload
    process("Hello");    // Calls the string overload
    return 0;
}
```

In the above program, we use **std::enable_if** and type traits to direct overload resolution. The **std::is_integral_v<T>** and **std::is_floating_point_v<T>** checks ensure that the correct overload is chosen based on whether the argument is an integral type (like **int** or **long**) or a floating-point type (like **float** or **double**). This technique is particularly useful when writing generic code that must handle a wide range of types but requires different behavior depending on the type of input.

Crafting Type-safe Solutions with Perfect Forwarding

To further enhance the flexibility of our overloaded functions, we can incorporate perfect forwarding. Perfect forwarding ensures that arguments are forwarded to the appropriate overloads without losing their original types or value categories.

Below, we will see how we can combine perfect forwarding with function overloading to create type-safe and efficient solutions:

```
#include <iostream>

#include <string>

#include <utility>

#include <type_traits>


// Overload for integers

template<typename T>

std::enable_if_t<std::is_integral_v<T>, void>

process(T&& x) {

    std::cout << "Processing integral: " <<
std::forward<T>(x) << std::endl;

}


// Overload for floating-point numbers

template<typename T>

std::enable_if_t<std::is_floating_point_v<T>, void>

process(T&& x) {

    std::cout << "Processing floating-point: " <<
std::forward<T>(x) << std::endl;

}
```

```
// Overload for strings
void process(const std::string& x) {
    std::cout << "Processing string: " << x << std::endl;
}

int main() {
    int x = 42;
    process(x);            // Calls the integral overload, 
lvalue
    process(3.14);         // Calls the floating-point 
overload, rvalue
    process("Hello");      // Calls the string overload, 
rvalue
    return 0;
}
```

In this version, we use perfect forwarding (**std::forward<T>(x)**) to ensure that the argument is forwarded to the correct overload without unnecessary copying. The **std::enable_if** checks ensure that the right overload is chosen based on the type of the argument, while perfect forwarding preserves the value category (whether it's an lvalue or an rvalue).

In complex systems, particularly when multiple layers of templates and type traits are involved, overload resolution can become tricky. In such cases, it's important to design functions that are robust enough to handle potential ambiguities while maintaining type safety and flexibility.

Dynamic Functions with 'std::function' and

Callables

Callable objects encompass anything that can be "called" as if it were a function—this includes regular functions, function pointers, lambdas, and functors (objects with overloaded **operator()**). The **std::function** class template provides a flexible wrapper that can hold any callable object, allowing functions to be passed around, stored, and invoked dynamically. This flexibility is particularly useful when you want to design code that adapts at runtime, as it allows you to create dynamic and highly reusable functions.

In this section, we will explore how **std::function** and callable objects can be used to build dynamic functions that can be passed as arguments, stored in containers, and invoked in various scenarios.

Introduction to 'std::function'

std::function is a polymorphic function wrapper, meaning it can store any callable entity that matches a specific function signature. This makes it incredibly versatile for dynamic programming, where you might want to store and call different functions depending on the context.

To see it in action, we will start with a simple example that demonstrates how **std::function** can be used to store and invoke a lambda function:

```
#include <iostream>

#include <functional>  // For std::function


int main() {

    // Define a lambda function

    auto lambda = [](int x, int y) -> int {

        return x + y;

    };


    // Store the lambda in a std::function
```

```
    std::function<int(int, int)> add = lambda;


    // Call the std::function

    std::cout << "Result: " << add(3, 4) << std::endl;
// Outputs: Result: 7


    return 0;

}
```

In the above sample script, we define a simple lambda function that takes two integers and returns their sum. We then store this lambda inside a **std::function** object named **add**, which is defined to match the lambda's signature: **int(int, int)**. Once the lambda is stored in **std::function**, it can be called just like a regular function.

The key advantage of **std::function** is its ability to hold any callable entity, not just lambdas. This includes regular functions, function pointers, and functors.

Storing and Passing Dynamic Functions

The flexibility of **std::function** allows you to dynamically switch between different functions at runtime. We will extend the example by introducing a regular function and demonstrating how both a function and a lambda can be stored in the same **std::function** and passed around dynamically.

```
#include <iostream>

#include <functional>


// A regular function

int multiply(int x, int y) {

    return x * y;
```

```
}


int main() {

    // Lambda function

    auto add = [](int x, int y) -> int {

        return x + y;

    };


    // std::function can store both a regular function
and a lambda

    std::function<int(int, int)> operation = add;

    std::cout << "Addition: " << operation(3, 4) <<
std::endl;  // Outputs: Addition: 7


    // Switch to the regular function

    operation = multiply;

    std::cout << "Multiplication: " << operation(3, 4) <<
std::endl;  // Outputs: Multiplication: 12


    return 0;

}
```

In the above sample script, we store two different types of callable objects (a lambda and a regular function) in the same **std::function**. The program first stores the lambda **add** in the

std::function and calls it to perform addition. Then, we switch the stored function to the regular **multiply** function and call it to perform multiplication.

Functors with 'std::function'

Functors, also known as function objects, are objects that can be called like functions. They achieve this by overloading the **operator()** in a class or struct. **std::function** can also store functors, providing another layer of flexibility.

Following is an example of how to use a functor with **std::function**:

```
#include <iostream>

#include <functional>


// A functor (function object) that performs subtraction

struct Subtract {

    int operator()(int x, int y) const {

        return x - y;

    }

};


int main() {

    // Define a functor object

    Subtract subtract;


    // Store the functor in a std::function

    std::function<int(int, int)> operation = subtract;
```

```
    std::cout << "Subtraction: " << operation(10, 4) <<
std::endl;  // Outputs: Subtraction: 6


    return 0;

}
```

In the above sample script, we define a functor **Subtract** that overloads the **operator()** to perform subtraction. We then store this functor in a **std::function** and invoke it just like any other function. This demonstrates the flexibility of **std::function**, as it can seamlessly handle functors in addition to lambdas and regular functions.

Passing Functions as Parameters

One of the most common uses of **std::function** is passing functions as parameters to other functions, allowing dynamic behavior to be injected into different parts of your program. We will create an example where we pass a function as a parameter to another function:

```
#include <iostream>

#include <functional>


// A higher-order function that accepts a callable object

void execute_operation(const std::function<int(int,
int)>& func, int a, int b) {

    std::cout << "Result: " << func(a, b) << std::endl;

}


int main() {

    // Lambda function to perform division
```

```
    auto divide = [](int x, int y) -> int {
        return y != 0 ? x / y : 0;  // Simple division
with a check for division by zero
    };

    // Call the higher-order function with a lambda
    execute_operation(divide, 20, 4);  // Outputs:
Result: 5

    return 0;
}
```

In the above program, the **execute_operation** function accepts a **std::function<int(int, int)>** as a parameter, allowing any callable object with that signature to be passed. We pass a lambda that performs division to **execute_operation**, and the lambda is invoked dynamically within the function. This approach makes the code more flexible and reusable, as you can pass different functions to **execute_operation** without changing its internal implementation.

Storing Functions in Containers

Another advantage of **std::function** is that it can be stored in containers, allowing you to build lists or maps of callable objects. This is particularly useful in scenarios where you need to store a collection of functions and invoke them dynamically based on conditions.

Following is an example where we store multiple **std::function** objects in a container and invoke them:

```
#include <iostream>

#include <functional>

#include <vector>
```

```
// A simple set of operations
int add(int x, int y) { return x + y; }
int subtract(int x, int y) { return x - y; }
int multiply(int x, int y) { return x * y; }

int main() {
    // Define a vector of std::function objects
    std::vector<std::function<int(int, int)>> operations;

    // Store different operations in the container
    operations.push_back(add);
    operations.push_back(subtract);
    operations.push_back(multiply);

    // Execute all the stored operations with the same
arguments
    for (const auto& operation : operations) {
        std::cout << "Result: " << operation(10, 5) <<
std::endl;
    }
```

```
    return 0;
}
```

In the above program, we define three functions (**add**, **subtract**, and **multiply**) and store them in a **std::vector** of **std::function**. We then loop through the container and invoke each function with the same arguments, and thereby it shows how you can use **std::function** to create collections of callable objects that can be invoked dynamically based on the situation.

'std::function' with Member Functions

In addition to handling free functions, lambdas, and functors, **std::function** can also store member functions of classes. When storing a member function, you need to pass both the object instance and the member function pointer.

Following is a sample program of how to use **std::function** with member functions:

```
#include <iostream>
#include <functional>

class Calculator {
public:
    int add(int x, int y) const {
        return x + y;
    }

    int multiply(int x, int y) const {
        return x * y;
    }
```

```
};

int main() {
    Calculator calc;

    // Store a member function in a std::function
    std::function<int(const Calculator&, int, int)>
operation;

    // Store and call the add member function
    operation = &Calculator::add;
    std::cout << "Addition: " << operation(calc, 3, 4) <<
std::endl;  // Outputs: Addition: 7

    // Store and call the multiply member function
    operation = &Calculator::multiply;
    std::cout << "Multiplication: " << operation(calc, 3,
4) << std::endl;  // Outputs: Multiplication: 12

    return 0;
}
```

In the above sample script, we store member functions **`add`** and **`multiply`** from the **`Calculator`** class inside a **`std::function`**. We pass the object **`calc`** to the

std::function when calling the member functions. This technique allows you to store and invoke member functions dynamically, further enhancing the flexibility of **std::function**. Whether you are working with lambdas, regular functions, functors, or member functions, **std::function** provides a unified interface for handling all types of callable objects.

Summary

In general, the goal was to make functions in C++23 more dynamic and flexible. At the outset of the chapter, we looked at how parameter packs can be utilized to morph functions, making them capable of easily handling functions with varying numbers of arguments. It was demonstrated through examples how to combine variadic templates with perfect forwarding to build adaptable APIs for various data types and quantities. We next turned our attention to lambdas, where we first heard of shape-shifting lambdas. These lambdas were shown to dynamically handle different types of arguments, which further increases the anonymous functions' flexibility. The examples showed how useful lambdas are for dynamic operations because they are callable objects that can handle different types of arguments.

The chapter concluded with an exploration of advanced function overloading, demonstrating how this technique could be extended to handle difficult cases like ambiguity and disambiguation. Overload resolution with type traits and other techniques were showcased, paving the way for the development of dynamic, type-safe solutions. It also demonstrated how to build dynamic, flexible systems with the ability to pass, store, and invoke functions at runtime through the detailed coverage of **std::function** and callable objects. This chapter covered all the bases when it came to working with functions, giving you the skills to write code that can change and adapt on the fly.

CHAPTER 3: TAMING LOW-LEVEL IO OPERATIONS

Overview

Acquiring proficiency in low-level I/O operations takes center stage in this chapter. The topics covered will allow you to have precise control over how your programs interact with files and data streams. We begin by looking at file descriptors, which are the basic building blocks of low-level I/O. You will learn how to precisely manage and manipulate file descriptors, allowing you to interact with file systems and resources at a deeper level than high-level abstractions allow.

Next, we will look at direct file manipulation, which goes beyond traditional file I/O. This section describes how to bypass the standard buffering mechanisms and directly access data, resulting in improved performance and fine-grained control over file operations. Next, we will optimize low-level I/O streams. You will learn how to streamline data transfer processes so that your I/O operations run faster and more efficiently.

Finally, we will go over advanced techniques for customizing stream buffers and fine-tuning I/O streams. By the end of this chapter, you will understand how to efficiently manage low-level I/O operations, giving you complete control over file and stream handling.

Dominate File Descriptors with Precision

A file descriptor is a small integer representing an open file, socket, or pipe. In low-level I/O operations, file descriptors are essential components for managing input and output in UNIX-like systems. C++23, while primarily high-level, integrates seamlessly with system-level resources like file descriptors, allowing you to interact with the operating system's I/O subsystem in a more direct and controlled way. File descriptors give you fine-grained control over how data is read from or written to these resources, allowing for non-blocking operations, resource monitoring, and more efficient handling of I/O in performance-critical applications. We will now explore some advanced techniques for mastering file descriptors.

Opening and Managing File Descriptors

One of the core operations when working with file descriptors is opening a file. While C++ streams use abstractions like **std::ifstream** and **std::ofstream** to handle file input and output, file descriptors offer a more direct way to interact with files using system calls like **open()** and **close()**. The **open()** function from **<fcntl.h>** is used to open a file and returns a file descriptor, which is an integer that serves as the handle for performing read/write operations on the file.

Following is a practical demonstration of how to open and manage file descriptors in C++:

```
#include <iostream>
```

```
#include <fcntl.h>  // For open()
#include <unistd.h> // For close()

int main() {
    // Open a file with read-only permissions
    int fd = open("example.txt", O_RDONLY);

    // Check if the file descriptor is valid
    if (fd == -1) {
        std::cerr << "Failed to open file" << std::endl;
        return 1;
    }

    std::cout << "File opened with file descriptor: " <<
fd << std::endl;

    // Perform operations with the file descriptor (e.g.,
reading, writing)

    // Close the file descriptor
    if (close(fd) == -1) {
```

```
        std::cerr << "Failed to close file descriptor" <<
std::endl;
        return 1;
    }

    std::cout << "File descriptor closed successfully" <<
std::endl;

    return 0;
}
```

In the above script, the **open()** function is used to open the file **example.txt** in read-only mode, returning a file descriptor. If the file is successfully opened, the file descriptor is printed, and later, it's closed using the **close()** function to release the system resources associated with it.

When working with file descriptors, it's crucial to ensure that they are properly managed—files must be closed to avoid resource leaks, and failing to close a file descriptor can lead to memory or resource exhaustion, especially in applications that open many files or connections.

Controlling File Access and Non-Blocking Operations

One of the most significant advantages of using file descriptors is the ability to control how files are accessed, and by passing different flags to the **open()** system call, you can dictate how the file should behave during I/O operations. For example, you can open files in read-only, write-only, or read-write modes.

The other concept, Non-blocking I/O means that when you attempt to read from or write to a file (or socket), the operation will not cause your program to wait if the data is not immediately available. Instead, the system returns immediately, allowing your program to continue executing other tasks. The file descriptors allow you to perform non-blocking I/O operations for performance-sensitive applications like networking servers or applications that require real-time responsiveness.

To understand better, we will modify our earlier example to demonstrate how to open a file in non-blocking mode:

```
#include <iostream>

#include <fcntl.h>

#include <unistd.h>


int main() {

    // Open the file in read-only and non-blocking mode

    int fd = open("example.txt", O_RDONLY | O_NONBLOCK);


    // Check if the file descriptor is valid

    if (fd == -1) {

        std::cerr << "Failed to open file in non-blocking
mode" << std::endl;

        return 1;

    }


    std::cout << "File opened in non-blocking mode with
file descriptor: " << fd << std::endl;


    // Perform non-blocking operations with the file
descriptor (e.g., read, write)
```

```
    // Close the file descriptor
    if (close(fd) == -1) {
        std::cerr << "Failed to close file descriptor" << std::endl;
        return 1;
    }

    std::cout << "File descriptor closed successfully" << std::endl;

    return 0;
}
```

Here, the **O_NONBLOCK** flag is passed to the **open()** function. This flag instructs the system to open the file in non-blocking mode, meaning that subsequent read/write operations won't block the program if data is unavailable. This technique is useful when you are dealing with large files, pipes, or sockets, where I/O latency can introduce delays.

Reading and Writing with File Descriptors

Once a file descriptor is opened, you can use the **read()** and **write()** system calls to perform I/O operations directly on the file. These system calls provide low-level access to the file system, allowing you to read and write raw data in a highly efficient manner. We will take a look at how you can read from and write to a file using file descriptors.

Given below is a sample program of reading data from a file using **read()**:

```
#include <iostream>
#include <fcntl.h>
#include <unistd.h>
```

```
int main() {
    // Open the file in read-only mode
    int fd = open("example.txt", O_RDONLY);

    if (fd == -1) {
        std::cerr << "Failed to open file" << std::endl;
        return 1;
    }

    // Buffer to store the data read from the file
    char buffer[128];

    // Read up to 128 bytes from the file descriptor
    ssize_t bytesRead = read(fd, buffer, sizeof(buffer) -
1);

    if (bytesRead == -1) {
        std::cerr << "Failed to read from file" <<
std::endl;
        close(fd);
        return 1;
```

```
    }

    // Null-terminate the buffer and print the contents
    buffer[bytesRead] = '\0';
    std::cout << "Read " << bytesRead << " bytes: " <<
buffer << std::endl;

    // Close the file descriptor
    close(fd);

    return 0;
}
```

In the above program, we open a file and use the **read()** system call to read up to 128 bytes of data into a buffer. The **read()** function returns the number of bytes successfully read, and the buffer is then printed to display the file's contents.

Similarly, writing to a file using a file descriptor is just as straightforward. Following is a sample program that demonstrates how to write data to a file:

```
#include <iostream>
#include <fcntl.h>
#include <unistd.h>

int main() {
```

```
    // Open the file in write-only mode (create the file
if it doesn't exist)
    int fd = open("output.txt", O_WRONLY | O_CREAT,
0644);

    if (fd == -1) {
        std::cerr << "Failed to open file for writing" <<
std::endl;
        return 1;
    }

    // Data to write to the file
    const char* data = "Hello, File Descriptors!";

    // Write the data to the file
    ssize_t bytesWritten = write(fd, data, strlen(data));

    if (bytesWritten == -1) {
        std::cerr << "Failed to write to file" <<
std::endl;
        close(fd);
        return 1;
    }
```

```
    std::cout << "Wrote " << bytesWritten << " bytes to
file" << std::endl;


    // Close the file descriptor

    close(fd);


    return 0;
}
```

In the above program, the **open()** function opens the file **output.txt** for writing. If the file doesn't exist, it is created with read/write permissions for the owner, and read permissions for the group and others (**0644**). The **write()** function writes the string **"Hello, File Descriptors!"** to the file, and we print the number of bytes written.

Handling File System Resources with Precision

File descriptors are not limited to file access—they can also represent other resources such as sockets, pipes, and devices, and managing these resources with precision is crucial in server applications or real-time systems where you have multiple I/O streams. One of the advanced techniques for handling file descriptors is using **select()** or **poll()** to monitor multiple file descriptors for events, such as data being available for reading or the ability to write without blocking.

Following is a brief demonstration of using **select()** to monitor multiple file descriptors:

```
#include <iostream>

#include <sys/select.h>

#include <fcntl.h>

#include <unistd.h>
```

```
int main() {
    // Open two files for monitoring
    int fd1 = open("file1.txt", O_RDONLY | O_NONBLOCK);
    int fd2 = open("file2.txt", O_RDONLY | O_NONBLOCK);

    if (fd1 == -1 || fd2 == -1) {
        std::cerr << "Failed to open files" << std::endl;
        return 1;
    }

    // Set up the file descriptor set
    fd_set readfds;
    FD_ZERO(&readfds);
    FD_SET(fd1, &readfds);
    FD_SET(fd2, &readfds);

    // Monitor both file descriptors for readability
    int max_fd = std::max(fd1, fd2);
    int result = select(max_fd + 1, &readfds, nullptr,
nullptr, nullptr);
```

```
    if (result == -1) {
        std::cerr << "Error with select()" << std::endl;
        close(fd1);
        close(fd2);
        return 1;
    }

    if (FD_ISSET(fd1, &readfds)) {
        std::cout << "Data available in file1.txt" <<
std::endl;
    }

    if (FD_ISSET(fd2, &readfds)) {
        std::cout << "Data available in file2.txt" <<
std::endl;
    }

    // Close the file descriptors
    close(fd1);
    close(fd2);

    return 0;
```

```
}
```

Here, the **select()** function is used to monitor two file descriptors (**fd1** and **fd2**). The program waits until either file becomes ready for reading. Overall, by means of precise control of file access modes, non-blocking operations, and direct system-level calls like **read()**, **write()**, and **select()**, you can optimize performance in environments where efficient I/O handling is very much needed.

Push Boundaries with Direct File Manipulation

Direct file manipulation at the byte level allows for precise control over how your program interacts with storage devices. This level of control becomes important when you need to fine-tune I/O performance, handle raw data efficiently, or access specific parts of a file without relying on high-level abstractions. In this section, we will focus on how to manipulate files directly by working with raw file descriptors, managing buffers, and gaining fine-grained control over file operations.

Direct file manipulation is particularly useful in performance-critical applications or when dealing with non-standard file formats, binary data, or low-level device interfaces. You can bypass the overhead of higher-level I/O abstractions (such as streams) and directly interact with the underlying file system, making it ideal for situations where you need full control over how data is read and written.

Reading and Writing Bytes at the Raw Level

At the core of direct file manipulation is the ability to work with raw bytes. Rather than using high-level file I/O mechanisms, we rely on system calls like **read()** and **write()** to perform operations at the byte level. By doing so, we can read or write exactly the number of bytes we want, starting from a specific offset, without relying on the automatic buffering that higher-level abstractions like **std::ifstream** or **std::ofstream** use.

Now here, we will start by writing a small program that reads and writes files directly at the byte level:

```
#include <iostream>

#include <fcntl.h>

#include <unistd.h>

#include <cstring>  // For memset()
```

```
int main() {
    // Open a file for reading and writing
    int fd = open("data.bin", O_RDWR | O_CREAT, 0644);

    if (fd == -1) {
        std::cerr << "Failed to open file" << std::endl;
        return 1;
    }

    // Buffer to hold the data
    char buffer[10];

    // Fill the buffer with the value 0xAA (just for
demonstration purposes)
    memset(buffer, 0xAA, sizeof(buffer));

    // Write the buffer to the file
    ssize_t bytesWritten = write(fd, buffer,
sizeof(buffer));

    if (bytesWritten == -1) {
```

```
        std::cerr << "Failed to write to file" <<
std::endl;
        close(fd);
        return 1;
    }

    std::cout << "Wrote " << bytesWritten << " bytes to
the file." << std::endl;

    // Set the file offset to the beginning of the file
    lseek(fd, 0, SEEK_SET);

    // Clear the buffer for reading
    memset(buffer, 0, sizeof(buffer));

    // Read data from the file
    ssize_t bytesRead = read(fd, buffer, sizeof(buffer));

    if (bytesRead == -1) {
        std::cerr << "Failed to read from file" <<
std::endl;
        close(fd);
```

```
        return 1;
    }

    std::cout << "Read " << bytesRead << " bytes from the
file." << std::endl;

    // Print the read data in hexadecimal format
    for (ssize_t i = 0; i < bytesRead; ++i) {
        std::cout << "0x" << std::hex << (int)(unsigned
char)buffer[i] << " ";
    }
    std::cout << std::endl;

    // Close the file descriptor
    close(fd);

    return 0;
}
```

In the above example, we open a binary file **data.bin** for reading and writing. We create a buffer of 10 bytes and fill it with the value **0xAA** (a pattern for illustrative purposes) using the **memset()** function. The **write()** system call is then used to write the contents of the buffer directly to the file, bypassing any high-level abstractions. After writing, we reset the file offset using **lseek()** to move the file pointer back to the beginning, and we use **read()** to read the data back into the buffer.

The output you get demonstrates the raw byte-level manipulation, showing exactly what is written to and read from the file in a hexadecimal format.

Managing Buffers for Direct File Manipulation

The buffer is essentially a memory space where data is temporarily stored before being written to or after being read from the file. The size and handling of buffers can significantly affect performance. For example, small buffer sizes might lead to more frequent system calls, increasing overhead, while larger buffers can reduce the number of calls but require more memory. Unlike higher-level I/O, where buffering is handled for you, direct file manipulation requires you to manage your own buffers.

We will enhance our program by allowing dynamic buffer management, where we allocate a buffer based on the size of the file:

```
#include <iostream>

#include <fcntl.h>

#include <unistd.h>

#include <sys/stat.h>  // For file size


int main() {

    // Open the file for reading

    int fd = open("data.bin", O_RDONLY);


    if (fd == -1) {

        std::cerr << "Failed to open file" << std::endl;

        return 1;

    }
```

```
    // Get the file size using fstat()
    struct stat fileInfo;
    if (fstat(fd, &fileInfo) == -1) {
        std::cerr << "Failed to get file size" <<
std::endl;
        close(fd);
        return 1;
    }

    off_t fileSize = fileInfo.st_size;
    std::cout << "File size: " << fileSize << " bytes" <<
std::endl;

    // Dynamically allocate buffer based on file size
    char* buffer = new char[fileSize];

    // Read the entire file into the buffer
    ssize_t bytesRead = read(fd, buffer, fileSize);

    if (bytesRead == -1) {
        std::cerr << "Failed to read from file" <<
std::endl;
```

```
        delete[] buffer;

        close(fd);

        return 1;

    }


    std::cout << "Read " << bytesRead << " bytes from the
file." << std::endl;


    // Print the read data in hexadecimal format

    for (ssize_t i = 0; i < bytesRead; ++i) {

        std::cout << "0x" << std::hex << (int)(unsigned
char)buffer[i] << " ";

    }

    std::cout << std::endl;


    // Clean up

    delete[] buffer;

    close(fd);


    return 0;

}
```

Here, we use **fstat()** to determine the size of the file **data.bin**, and then we dynamically allocate a buffer large enough to hold the entire contents of the file. This approach gives you control over buffer size and memory usage, ensuring that you can optimize performance based on file size and memory constraints.

Seeking and Manipulating File Offsets

Another important aspect of direct file manipulation is controlling the file offset. This capability is crucial for random-access file operations, such as manipulating specific records in a large database file or updating parts of a binary file.

Following is a sample program demonstrating how to move the file pointer to different locations and manipulate specific bytes:

```
#include <iostream>

#include <fcntl.h>

#include <unistd.h>


int main() {

    // Open the file for reading and writing

    int fd = open("data.bin", O_RDWR);


    if (fd == -1) {

        std::cerr << "Failed to open file" << std::endl;

        return 1;

    }


    // Seek to the 5th byte in the file

    if (lseek(fd, 5, SEEK_SET) == -1) {
```

```
        std::cerr << "Failed to seek to position" <<
std::endl;
        close(fd);
        return 1;
    }

    // Read 1 byte from the 5th byte position
    char byte;
    if (read(fd, &byte, 1) == -1) {
        std::cerr << "Failed to read byte" << std::endl;
        close(fd);
        return 1;
    }

    std::cout << "Byte at position 5: 0x" << std::hex <<
(int)(unsigned char)byte << std::endl;

    // Modify the byte and write it back
    byte = 0xFF;  // Change the value to 0xFF
    lseek(fd, 5, SEEK_SET);  // Move back to the 5th byte
    if (write(fd, &byte, 1) == -1) {
        std::cerr << "Failed to write byte" << std::endl;
```

```
        close(fd);

        return 1;

    }


    std::cout << "Modified byte at position 5." <<
std::endl;


    // Close the file descriptor

    close(fd);


    return 0;

}
```

In the above example, we use **lseek()** to move the file pointer to the 5th byte in the file. We then read the byte at that position, modify it to **0xFF**, and write the new value back to the file. This technique is commonly used in low-level device interactions or when working with custom file formats that require precise positioning within the file.

Direct Interaction with Storage Devices

In addition to working with regular files, direct file manipulation techniques can be applied to interact with raw storage devices. For example, in UNIX-like systems, storage devices such as hard drives are treated as files, and you can open them using file descriptors and perform byte-level I/O operations. This is useful when building utilities like disk partitions, file system checkers, or low-level device drivers.

Given below is a quick illustration of how you might open and read from a raw storage device:

```
#include <iostream>

#include <fcntl.h>
```

```
#include <unistd.h>

int main() {
    // Open the raw device (replace with the actual
device path, e.g., /dev/sda)
    int fd = open("/dev/sda", O_RDONLY);

    if (fd == -1) {
        std::cerr << "Failed to open the device" <<
std::endl;
        return 1;
    }

    // Read the first 512 bytes (typically the size of a
sector)
    char buffer[512];
    if (read(fd, buffer, sizeof(buffer)) == -1) {
        std::cerr << "Failed to read from device" <<
std::endl;
        close(fd);
        return 1;
    }
```

```
    std::cout << "Read 512 bytes from the device." <<
std::endl;


    // Print the first 16 bytes in hexadecimal format

    for (int i = 0; i < 16; ++i) {

        std::cout << "0x" << std::hex << (int)(unsigned
char)buffer[i] << " ";

    }

    std::cout << std::endl;


    // Close the device

    close(fd);


    return 0;

}
```

In the above illustration, we open the raw device **/dev/** and read the first 512 bytes, which typically corresponds to one sector. This is a simple illustration to perform direct byte-level I/O on storage devices and gives you complete control over how you interact with the hardware.

Streamline Low-Level IO Streams

Overview of Low-Level IO Streams

Low-level I/O streams refer to direct and unbuffered interactions with files, sockets, and other system resources, typically using file descriptors or other system-specific identifiers. C++ offers high-level I/O abstractions such as **std::ifstream** and **std::ofstream** for file input/output operations. These are often used for text or binary data, offering automatic buffering, type safety, and ease of use. On the other hand, low-level I/O operations (like those using **read()**, **write()**, and file descriptors) provide more control over performance but lack the convenience of high-level I/O.

When working with low-level I/O streams, we typically deal with raw data, unformatted and unbuffered. This gives us more control over how data is processed, but it also requires more manual management of buffers, file descriptors, and error handling. However, when we need to interact with libraries or parts of the application that require C++ stream-based APIs (such as **std::ostream** or **std::istream**), we can streamline the interaction by combining low-level operations with C++ streams.

To achieve this, we need to understand how C++ streams work internally. In the following sample program, we create a custom stream buffer class that reads from and writes to a file descriptor. This allows us to use C++ streams (**std::istream**, **std::ostream**) for file I/O while retaining the low-level control that file descriptors offer.

Sample Program: Wrapping File Descriptors in Stream Buffers

Given below is how you can implement this:

```
#include <iostream>

#include <streambuf>

#include <unistd.h>

#include <fcntl.h>


// Custom stream buffer that works with file descriptors

class FdStreamBuffer : public std::streambuf {

public:

    FdStreamBuffer(int fd) : fd_(fd) {

        setg(in_buffer_, in_buffer_, in_buffer_);

        setp(out_buffer_, out_buffer_ + buffer_size_);
```

```
    }

protected:
    // Override underflow() to handle reading from the
file descriptor
    int underflow() override {
        if (gptr() == egptr()) {  // Check if the buffer
is empty
            ssize_t bytesRead = read(fd_, in_buffer_,
buffer_size_);
            if (bytesRead <= 0) {
                return traits_type::eof();  // Return EOF
if no more data is available
            }
            setg(in_buffer_, in_buffer_, in_buffer_ +
bytesRead);
        }
        return traits_type::to_int_type(*gptr());
    }

    // Override overflow() to handle writing to the file
descriptor
    int overflow(int ch) override {
```

```
        if (ch != traits_type::eof()) {
            *pptr() = ch;
            pbump(1);
        }
        return sync() == 0 ? ch : traits_type::eof();
    }

    // Override sync() to flush the buffer to the file
descriptor
    int sync() override {
        ssize_t bytesWritten = write(fd_, pbase(), pptr()
- pbase());
        if (bytesWritten < 0) {
            return -1;  // Return -1 on error
        }
        setp(out_buffer_, out_buffer_ + buffer_size_);
        return 0;
    }

private:
    static constexpr std::size_t buffer_size_ = 1024;
    int fd_;
```

```
    char in_buffer_[buffer_size_];

    char out_buffer_[buffer_size_];

};


// Helper function to create an input stream for a file
descriptor

std::istream createInputStream(int fd) {

    static FdStreamBuffer buffer(fd);

    return std::istream(&buffer);

}


// Helper function to create an output stream for a file
descriptor

std::ostream createOutputStream(int fd) {

    static FdStreamBuffer buffer(fd);

    return std::ostream(&buffer);

}


int main() {

    // Open a file using file descriptors

    int fd = open("example.txt", O_RDWR | O_CREAT, 0644);
```

```
    if (fd == -1) {
        std::cerr << "Failed to open file" << std::endl;
        return 1;
    }

    // Create C++ input and output streams using the
custom buffer
    std::istream in = createInputStream(fd);
    std::ostream out = createOutputStream(fd);

    // Write data to the file using the output stream
    out << "Writing data using std::ostream with file
descriptor integration!" << std::endl;
    out.flush();  // Ensure data is written to the file

    // Reset the file pointer to the beginning
    lseek(fd, 0, SEEK_SET);

    // Read data from the file using the input stream
    std::string line;
    std::getline(in, line);
    std::cout << "Read from file: " << line << std::endl;
```

```
    // Close the file descriptor
    close(fd);

    return 0;
}
```

In the above program, we created a custom stream buffer class **FdStreamBuffer** that handles low-level file descriptor operations. The class overrides the key functions of **std::streambuf** to manage reading from and writing to a file descriptor as detailed above:

Reading with 'underflow()'

This method is called when the input buffer is empty. It reads data from the file descriptor into an internal buffer and provides this data to the input stream. If there's no more data to read (EOF), it returns **traits_type::eof()** to signal the end of the input.

Writing with 'overflow()'

This method handles writing a single character to the output buffer. If the buffer is full, it flushes the contents to the file descriptor and resets the buffer.

Flushing with 'sync()'

When the output buffer is full or when the stream is explicitly flushed, **sync()** writes the buffered data to the file descriptor using the **write()** system call.

This whole integration of low-level control with high-level ease of use offers the best of both worlds. You gain access to raw file descriptor operations while also benefiting from the flexibility and ease of C++ stream abstractions. This is particularly useful in applications that require both performance and the convenience of high-level I/O handling, such as logging systems, network servers, and data processing pipelines.

Advanced Stream Buffers and IOStream Customization

We now turn our focus to mastering stream buffer management, particularly in high-I/O environments where performance optimization is crucial. C++ streams, at their core, are backed by the **std::streambuf** class, which handles the actual input and output operations. When working in high-I/O environments—such as file servers, network applications, or large data processing systems—efficient buffer management can significantly affect throughput and performance.

In this topic, we will first explore how mastering stream buffer management can optimize performance, and then we will learn to customize **std::streambuf** for specific I/O demands or needs.

Stream Buffer Management for Performance

In high-I/O environments, a poorly managed buffer can lead to frequent and unnecessary I/O operations, which degrade performance. Conversely, a well-managed buffer minimizes these operations, allowing you to read or write larger chunks of data at once, reducing overhead and increasing throughput.

To demonstrate this, we will revisit the custom **FdStreamBuffer** class from the previous topic and modify it for better performance in a high-I/O scenario.

```
#include <iostream>

#include <streambuf>

#include <unistd.h>

#include <fcntl.h>


class HighPerformanceStreamBuffer : public std::streambuf
{

public:

    HighPerformanceStreamBuffer(int fd, std::size_t
bufferSize = 8192)

        : fd_(fd), buffer_size_(bufferSize), buffer_(new
char[bufferSize]) {
```

```
        setg(buffer_.get(), buffer_.get(),
buffer_.get());

        setp(buffer_.get(), buffer_.get() +
buffer_size_);

    }


    ~HighPerformanceStreamBuffer() {

        sync();  // Ensure any pending output is flushed

    }


protected:

    // Handle reading from the file descriptor into the
buffer

    int underflow() override {

        if (gptr() == egptr()) {  // Check if the get
area is empty

            ssize_t bytesRead = read(fd_, buffer_.get(),
buffer_size_);

            if (bytesRead <= 0) {

                return traits_type::eof();  // End of
file or error

            }

            setg(buffer_.get(), buffer_.get(),
buffer_.get() + bytesRead);
```

```
        }
        return traits_type::to_int_type(*gptr());
    }

    // Handle writing from the buffer to the file
descriptor
    int overflow(int ch) override {
        if (ch != traits_type::eof()) {
            *pptr() = ch;
            pbump(1);
        }
        return sync() == 0 ? ch : traits_type::eof();
    }

    // Flush the buffer to the file descriptor
    int sync() override {
        ssize_t bytesWritten = write(fd_, pbase(), pptr()
- pbase());
        if (bytesWritten < 0) {
            return -1;  // Error during write
        }
```

```
        setp(buffer_.get(), buffer_.get() +
buffer_size_);

        return 0;

    }


private:

    int fd_;

    std::size_t buffer_size_;

    std::unique_ptr<char[]> buffer_;

};


// Helper functions to create input and output streams

std::istream createHighPerformanceInputStream(int fd,
std::size_t bufferSize = 8192) {

    static HighPerformanceStreamBuffer buffer(fd,
bufferSize);

    return std::istream(&buffer);

}


std::ostream createHighPerformanceOutputStream(int fd,
std::size_t bufferSize = 8192) {

    static HighPerformanceStreamBuffer buffer(fd,
bufferSize);
```

```
    return std::ostream(&buffer);
}

int main() {
    // Open a file with file descriptors
    int fd = open("largefile.txt", O_RDWR | O_CREAT,
0644);

    if (fd == -1) {
        std::cerr << "Failed to open file" << std::endl;
        return 1;
    }

    // Create high-performance streams with a large
buffer size
    std::istream in =
createHighPerformanceInputStream(fd, 16384);  // 16KB
buffer for input
    std::ostream out =
createHighPerformanceOutputStream(fd, 16384);  // 16KB
buffer for output

    // Writing data to the file
```

```
    out << "This is a large file. Writing efficiently
with a custom stream buffer!" << std::endl;
    out.flush();  // Ensure data is written


    // Reset file pointer to the beginning
    lseek(fd, 0, SEEK_SET);


    // Reading data from the file
    std::string line;
    std::getline(in, line);
    std::cout << "Read from file: " << line << std::endl;


    // Close the file descriptor
    close(fd);


    return 0;
}
```

In the above program, we've enhanced the **FdStreamBuffer** to handle larger buffer sizes, which is important in high-I/O environments where reading or writing small chunks of data can lead to performance bottlenecks. The buffer is dynamically allocated based on the **bufferSize** parameter. In the **main()** function, we create high-performance input and output streams with a buffer size of 16KB for both reading and writing. This significantly improves performance when working with large files or high-throughput environments, as the I/O operations are batched into larger chunks.

Customizing 'std::streambuf' for Complex I/O

In addition to managing buffers for performance, customizing **`std::streambuf`** allows you to handle unique I/O scenarios that the standard stream classes might not accommodate. For example, you might need to:

- read from a combination of files, sockets, or in-memory buffers.
- create a stream buffer that reads from one source and writes to another, such as a network stream that reads from a file and writes to a socket.
- manipulate or filter data as it's being read or written, such as compressing data before writing it to a file.

For this, we will now create a custom **`std::streambuf`** that reads from multiple input sources, such as two different files, and interleaves their data into a single stream.

```
#include <iostream>

#include <streambuf>

#include <unistd.h>

#include <fcntl.h>


// Custom stream buffer to read from two different file
descriptors

class InterleavedStreamBuffer : public std::streambuf {

public:

    InterleavedStreamBuffer(int fd1, int fd2)

        : fd1_(fd1), fd2_(fd2), current_fd_(fd1_) {

        setg(buffer_, buffer_, buffer_);

    }
```

```
protected:

    // Read data from the two files in an interleaved
manner

    int underflow() override {

        if (gptr() == egptr()) {  // Buffer is empty

            ssize_t bytesRead = read(current_fd_,
buffer_, buffer_size_);

            if (bytesRead <= 0) {

                return traits_type::eof();  // EOF or
error

            }

            setg(buffer_, buffer_, buffer_ + bytesRead);


            // Switch between the two file descriptors
for interleaved reading

            current_fd_ = (current_fd_ == fd1_) ? fd2_ :
fd1_;

        }

        return traits_type::to_int_type(*gptr());

    }


private:

    static constexpr std::size_t buffer_size_ = 1024;
```

```
    int fd1_, fd2_;

    int current_fd_;

    char buffer_[buffer_size_];

};


// Helper function to create an input stream for
interleaved reading

std::istream createInterleavedInputStream(int fd1, int
fd2) {

    static InterleavedStreamBuffer buffer(fd1, fd2);

    return std::istream(&buffer);

}


int main() {

    // Open two files for reading

    int fd1 = open("file1.txt", O_RDONLY);

    int fd2 = open("file2.txt", O_RDONLY);


    if (fd1 == -1 || fd2 == -1) {

        std::cerr << "Failed to open files" << std::endl;

        return 1;

    }
```

```
    // Create an input stream that interleaves data from
both files
    std::istream in = createInterleavedInputStream(fd1,
fd2);

    // Read data from the interleaved stream
    std::string line;
    while (std::getline(in, line)) {
        std::cout << "Interleaved line: " << line <<
std::endl;
    }

    // Close file descriptors
    close(fd1);
    close(fd2);

    return 0;
}
```

In the above program, we created a custom **InterleavedStreamBuffer** that reads from two file descriptors (**fd1_** and **fd2_**) in an alternating or interleaved fashion. Each time the buffer is empty, it reads data from one file, then switches to the other file for the next read. This allowed you to interleave data from multiple sources into a single input stream.

Whether you are optimizing performance in high-I/O environments, interleaving data from multiple sources, or transforming data on the fly, customizing **std::streambuf** gives you full control over how input and output are handled in your application. This enables you to build advanced, efficient systems that perform well even under demanding conditions.

Summary

Ultimately, this chapter looked into the inner workings of C++'s low-level I/O operations and how they can be used to attain exact control over file handling. The main idea was to learn about file descriptors and how they let you edit files directly at the byte level. Through hands-on examples, it was demonstrated that file descriptors provide a more comprehensive, system-level way to work with files, enabling efficient reading and writing, precise control over file offsets, and operation without blocking.

The chapter also discussed buffer management for high-performance I/O. We learned how to use custom **std::streambuf** implementations to combine low-level file descriptors with higher-level C++ streams. The chapter also covered customizing **std::streambuf** for specific input and output scenarios, such as interleaving data from multiple sources and managing performance-critical streams. Overall, the chapter provided extensive advice on mastering stream buffers, optimizing performance in I/O-intensive applications, and customizing C++ stream handling for specific, complex scenarios.

Chapter 4: Mastering Buffering and Async IO

Overview

Improving data handling and performance in modern applications requires a solid grasp of advanced topics like asynchronous I/O (Input/Output) operations and buffering, which are covered in this chapter. We begin by looking at the mechanics of deep buffering, which explains how buffers manage data flow between various system components such as memory and storage devices. You will gain a better understanding of how effective buffering strategies can reduce latency while increasing throughput, ensuring that your programs handle large amounts of data efficiently.

The chapter then digs into asynchronous (or async) I/O operations. Here, you will learn how to do non-blocking I/O, which allows your programs to handle other tasks while data transfers complete. We will also push the boundaries of data transfer with Direct I/O. Finally, the chapter shows how to achieve I/O performance using asynchronous streams, which combines the advantages of asynchronous operations with efficient data handling in stream-based applications.

Dive into Deep Buffering Mechanics

In many applications, I/O operations are a significant bottleneck because devices like disks and networks are much slower than the CPU and memory. Proper buffer management allows the system to transfer data in larger chunks, reducing the number of system calls, and thus improving performance. In this section, we will dive into the mechanics of how buffering works, focusing on how you can tune buffer sizes and apply different strategies to optimize performance for various types of I/O operations.

Buffering Techniques

There are several buffering strategies that can be used depending on the type of I/O operation and the performance requirements of your system. These include:

Full Buffering

In full buffering, data is stored in a buffer until the buffer is full, and then it is written to or read from the I/O device in a single operation. This minimizes the number of I/O operations by transferring larger blocks of data at once, reducing the overhead associated with frequent system calls.

Line Buffering

This technique is used primarily in text-based I/O, where the buffer is flushed after each line is processed. This is commonly used in interactive applications where immediate feedback is required after each input line (such as in command-line programs).

No Buffering

In no buffering (or unbuffered) I/O, data is transferred directly between the application and the I/O device. While this offers the most direct control over the I/O operation, it comes at the cost of frequent, smaller data transfers that can negatively impact performance.

Buffer size plays a critical role in buffering efficiency. If the buffer is too small, the program will frequently pause to transfer data between the buffer and the I/O device, leading to higher overhead. On the other hand, if the buffer is too large, memory usage can increase unnecessarily, and the delay before flushing data might become excessive.

Sample Program: Tuning Buffer Sizes for Optimized I/O

Here, we will create a program that reads and writes data to a file, adjusting the buffer size to see its impact on performance. We will use the **`std::setvbuf()`** function, which allows you to control the buffering mode and size for a **`FILE`** stream in C++.

```
#include <iostream>

#include <cstdio>  // For FILE and setvbuf()

#include <cstdlib> // For malloc()

#include <chrono>  // For measuring performance


void write_data(FILE* file, const char* data, size_t
data_size) {

    size_t written = fwrite(data, sizeof(char),
data_size, file);

    if (written != data_size) {

        std::cerr << "Failed to write all data!" <<
std::endl;

    }

}
```

```
int main() {
    const char* file_name = "buffer_test.txt";
    const char* data = "This is some data being written
to the file.";
    size_t data_size = std::strlen(data);

    // Open the file for writing
    FILE* file = fopen(file_name, "w");
    if (!file) {
        std::cerr << "Failed to open file!" << std::endl;
        return 1;
    }

    // Set the buffer size to 4KB
    size_t buffer_size = 4096;
    char* buffer =
static_cast<char*>(std::malloc(buffer_size));

    // Measure the time taken for full buffering with a
custom buffer size
```

```
    auto start =
std::chrono::high_resolution_clock::now();

    if (setvbuf(file, buffer, _IOFBF, buffer_size) != 0)
{  // Full buffering mode

        std::cerr << "Failed to set buffer!" <<
std::endl;

        return 1;

    }

    write_data(file, data, data_size);

    fflush(file);  // Ensure data is written to disk

    auto end = std::chrono::high_resolution_clock::now();

    std::chrono::duration<double> full_buffer_duration =
end - start;

    std::cout << "Full buffering (4KB) time: " <<
full_buffer_duration.count() << " seconds" << std::endl;


    // Reset file for next test

    fclose(file);

    file = fopen(file_name, "w");


    // Line buffering test

    start = std::chrono::high_resolution_clock::now();
```

```
    if (setvbuf(file, buffer, _IOLBF, buffer_size) != 0)
{  // Line buffering mode

        std::cerr << "Failed to set buffer!" <<
std::endl;

        return 1;

    }

    write_data(file, data, data_size);

    fflush(file);  // Ensure data is written to disk

    end = std::chrono::high_resolution_clock::now();

    std::chrono::duration<double> line_buffer_duration =
end - start;

    std::cout << "Line buffering (4KB) time: " <<
line_buffer_duration.count() << " seconds" << std::endl;


    // Reset file for next test

    fclose(file);

    file = fopen(file_name, "w");


    // No buffering test

    start = std::chrono::high_resolution_clock::now();

    if (setvbuf(file, nullptr, _IONBF, 0) != 0) {  // No
buffering mode
```

```
        std::cerr << "Failed to set buffer!" <<
std::endl;
        return 1;
    }
    write_data(file, data, data_size);
    fflush(file);  // Ensure data is written to disk
    end = std::chrono::high_resolution_clock::now();
    std::chrono::duration<double> no_buffer_duration =
end - start;
    std::cout << "No buffering time: " <<
no_buffer_duration.count() << " seconds" << std::endl;

    // Clean up
    fclose(file);
    std::free(buffer);

    return 0;
}
```

In the above code,

- The program uses **`setvbuf()`** to change the buffering mode for a **`FILE`** stream. There are three buffering modes:
    - **`_IOFBF`** for full buffering (the buffer is flushed only when it's full),
    - **`_IOLBF`** for line buffering (the buffer is flushed after each line of output), and

    - **_IONBF** for no buffering (data is written directly to the I/O device).

- We manually allocate a buffer of 4KB (4096 bytes) using **std::malloc()** and pass it to **setvbuf()** in full and line buffering modes. This allows us to control the buffer size and evaluate its impact on performance.
- The program measures the time taken for each buffering mode by using **std::chrono** to record the duration of each operation. This helps illustrate how buffer size and mode affect performance during I/O operations.
- The program writes a small string to the file in each buffering mode. After writing, it calls **fflush()** to ensure that any buffered data is flushed to the disk.

When you run this program, you should observe different performance characteristics depending on the buffering mode:

- **Full Buffering (4KB):** Full buffering minimizes the number of writes to the disk by accumulating data in the buffer until it's full. This is often the most efficient mode for large I/O operations, as it reduces the overhead of frequent system calls.
- **Line Buffering (4KB):** Line buffering forces a flush after each newline, which can be useful in interactive applications but may degrade performance for large I/O operations due to more frequent writes.
- **No Buffering:** In no buffering mode, each write operation is immediately transferred to the disk without any intermediate buffering. This results in many small write operations, which can severely degrade performance, especially in systems where I/O is the bottleneck.

Excel Async I/O

Overview of Asynchronous I/O

Asynchronous I/O (also known as async I/O) allows programs to handle multiple I/O tasks concurrently without blocking the main thread. This is useful in high-performance and real-time applications, where I/O operations—such as reading from or writing to a file or network socket—can be slow due to waiting on external systems or resources. Now, the key to mastering asynchronous I/O is understanding how non-blocking I/O works, which we have learned in the previous chapter. Here, we will implement non-blocking I/O using system calls like **select()**, **poll()**, and **epoll()** to build a simple asynchronous I/O system.

Before diving into the implementation, we will briefly outline the basic concepts behind async I/O:

- **Multiplexing I/O Operations**: To handle multiple I/O streams concurrently, we use multiplexing mechanisms like **select()**, **poll()**, and **epoll()**. These system calls allow us to monitor multiple file descriptors (representing files, sockets, etc.) simultaneously and react when one of them is ready for reading or writing.
- **Event-driven programming:** Asynchronous I/O often follows an event-driven model, where the program waits for events (such as data being ready to read) and reacts accordingly, rather than continuously polling or blocking on I/O operations.

Sample Program: Non-blocking I/O using 'select()'

We will start by implementing a simple non-blocking I/O system using the **select()** system call. **select()** allows us to monitor multiple file descriptors (e.g., sockets or files) and wait until one or more of them are ready for I/O operations. Once a file descriptor is ready (e.g., data is available to read), we can process the I/O without blocking the entire program.

In the above sample script, we will use non-blocking I/O to read from multiple file descriptors simultaneously, simulating a scenario where the program is handling multiple I/O streams concurrently. We will use the **O_NONBLOCK** flag to set the file descriptors to non-blocking mode.

```
#include <iostream>

#include <fcntl.h>      // For open() and O_NONBLOCK

#include <unistd.h>     // For read(), write(), and
close()

#include <sys/select.h> // For select()

#include <cstring>      // For memset()


int main() {

    // Open two files for reading (use non-blocking mode)

    int fd1 = open("file1.txt", O_RDONLY | O_NONBLOCK);

    int fd2 = open("file2.txt", O_RDONLY | O_NONBLOCK);
```

```
    if (fd1 == -1 || fd2 == -1) {
        std::cerr << "Failed to open files in non-
blocking mode" << std::endl;
        return 1;
    }

    // Set up the file descriptor set for select()
    fd_set readfds;
    int max_fd = std::max(fd1, fd2);  // We need the
highest file descriptor value for select()

    char buffer[256];  // Buffer to store the data read
from the files
    bool fd1_done = false, fd2_done = false;  // Flags to
track if files are done

    // Main loop to monitor both files for reading
    while (!fd1_done || !fd2_done) {
        FD_ZERO(&readfds);  // Clear the set
        if (!fd1_done) FD_SET(fd1, &readfds);  // Add fd1
to the set if not done
        if (!fd2_done) FD_SET(fd2, &readfds);  // Add fd2
to the set if not done
```

```
        // Use select() to wait until one of the file
descriptors is ready to read
        int activity = select(max_fd + 1, &readfds,
nullptr, nullptr, nullptr);

        if (activity == -1) {
            std::cerr << "Error with select()" <<
std::endl;
            break;
        }

        // Check if fd1 is ready to read
        if (FD_ISSET(fd1, &readfds)) {
            ssize_t bytesRead = read(fd1, buffer,
sizeof(buffer) - 1);
            if (bytesRead > 0) {
                buffer[bytesRead] = '\0';  // Null-
terminate the buffer
                std::cout << "Read from file1.txt: " <<
buffer << std::endl;
            } else if (bytesRead == 0) {
                fd1_done = true;  // End of file
```

```
                std::cout << "file1.txt is done." <<
std::endl;
            } else {
                std::cerr << "Error reading from
file1.txt" << std::endl;
            }
        }

        // Check if fd2 is ready to read
        if (FD_ISSET(fd2, &readfds)) {
            ssize_t bytesRead = read(fd2, buffer,
sizeof(buffer) - 1);
            if (bytesRead > 0) {
                buffer[bytesRead] = '\0';
                std::cout << "Read from file2.txt: " <<
buffer << std::endl;
            } else if (bytesRead == 0) {
                fd2_done = true;  // End of file
                std::cout << "file2.txt is done." <<
std::endl;
            } else {
                std::cerr << "Error reading from
file2.txt" << std::endl;
```

```
            }
        }
    }

    // Clean up
    close(fd1);
    close(fd2);

    return 0;
}
```

In the above snippet,

- We open two files (**file1.txt** and **file2.txt**) in non-blocking mode using the **O_NONBLOCK** flag. This allows the program to continue running without waiting for the **read()** system call to complete. If there's no data available, **read()** returns immediately without blocking.
- We then use the **select()** system call to monitor both file descriptors (**fd1** and **fd2**). **select()** allows us to check if any of the file descriptors are ready for reading, writing, or have encountered an error. The program blocks on **select()** until one of the file descriptors is ready.
- Next, inside the loop, we use **FD_SET()** to add the file descriptors to the **readfds** set, which **select()** monitors for readability. When **select()** returns, we check which file descriptor is ready using **FD_ISSET()**. If **fd1** or **fd2** is ready, we read from it and process the data.
- And finally, the **read()** system call attempts to read data from the file without blocking. If data is available, it reads into the buffer and prints the result. If the file is done (i.e., no more data to read), we set a flag to stop monitoring that file.

This approach demonstrates how to use non-blocking I/O to handle multiple I/O tasks concurrently in a single thread, without blocking the program while waiting for data to become available. This is particularly useful in server applications, where multiple clients may be connected simultaneously, or in real-time systems where responsiveness is critical.

Sample Program: Non-blocking I/O with Network Sockets

The previous example dealt with files, but non-blocking I/O is particularly useful in networking, where communication with clients and servers can involve unpredictable delays. Here, we will demonstrate how to use non-blocking I/O with sockets, allowing a server to handle multiple clients simultaneously.

```
#include <iostream>

#include <cstring>

#include <sys/socket.h>

#include <arpa/inet.h>

#include <fcntl.h>

#include <unistd.h>

#include <sys/select.h>


int main() {

    // Create a TCP socket

    int server_fd = socket(AF_INET, SOCK_STREAM, 0);

    if (server_fd == -1) {

        std::cerr << "Failed to create socket" <<
std::endl;

        return 1;

    }
```

```
    // Bind the socket to a port
    sockaddr_in server_addr{};
    server_addr.sin_family = AF_INET;
    server_addr.sin_port = htons(8080);
    server_addr.sin_addr.s_addr = INADDR_ANY;
    if (bind(server_fd, (struct sockaddr*)&server_addr,
sizeof(server_addr)) == -1) {
        std::cerr << "Failed to bind socket" <<
std::endl;
        close(server_fd);
        return 1;
    }

    // Listen for incoming connections
    if (listen(server_fd, 5) == -1) {
        std::cerr << "Failed to listen on socket" <<
std::endl;
        close(server_fd);
        return 1;
    }

    // Set the server socket to non-blocking mode
```

```
    fcntl(server_fd, F_SETFL, O_NONBLOCK);


    fd_set readfds;
    int max_fd = server_fd;
    sockaddr_in client_addr{};
    socklen_t client_len = sizeof(client_addr);


    std::cout << "Server is listening on port 8080..." <<
std::endl;


    // Main loop to handle incoming connections and data
    while (true) {
        FD_ZERO(&readfds);
        FD_SET(server_fd, &readfds);


        // Monitor the server socket for new connections
        int activity = select(max_fd + 1, &readfds,
nullptr, nullptr, nullptr);


        if (activity == -1) {
            std::cerr << "Error with select()" <<
std::endl;
```

```
            break;
        }

        // Check if the server socket is ready to accept
a new connection
        if (FD_ISSET(server_fd, &readfds)) {
            int client_fd = accept(server_fd, (struct
sockaddr*)&client_addr, &client_len);
            if (client_fd == -1) {
                std::cerr << "Failed to accept
connection" << std::endl;
            } else {
                // Set the client socket to non-blocking
mode
                fcntl(client_fd, F_SETFL, O_NONBLOCK);
                std::cout << "New client connected" <<
std::endl;

                // Handle the client connection
                close(client_fd);
            }
        }
    }
```

```
    // Close the server socket

    close(server_fd);


    return 0;

}
```

In the above script,

- We create a TCP server socket and set it to non-blocking mode using **fcntl()** with the **O_NONBLOCK** flag. This allows the server to continue processing without blocking on **accept()**.
- Similar to the file example, we use **select()** to monitor the server socket for new connections. When a client attempts to connect, **select()** returns, and we call **accept()** to establish the connection. In non-blocking mode, **accept()** returns immediately, even if no clients are waiting.
- Once a client connects, we can set the client's socket to non-blocking mode as well, allowing the server to handle multiple clients without blocking on any one client's I/O.

This approach is for scalable, high-performance servers that can handle multiple clients concurrently. The use of non-blocking I/O and **select()** helps to manage multiple connections without dedicating a separate thread or process for each client.

With this, we learnt to design systems that handle multiple I/O tasks concurrently especially in high-performance or real-time environments. These techniques form the basis for scalable servers, network applications, and any system requiring efficient I/O management.

Push Data Transfer Limits with Direct IO

After learning how to manage asynchronous I/O, now we turn to Direct I/O and advanced techniques like memory-mapped I/O (MMIO) and zero-copy mechanisms, which provide even more efficient data transfer methods.

What is Direct I/O?

In a typical I/O operation, data passes through the operating system's buffer cache, where it is temporarily stored before being written to or read from the disk. While this is efficient for most general-purpose applications, there are situations where bypassing these buffers and directly accessing the disk or device can significantly improve performance.

Direct I/O allows us to bypass the operating system's caching mechanisms and write or read data directly to or from disk. This can reduce memory usage (since there is no need for an extra copy of the data in the kernel buffers) and improve performance, particularly in cases where the application already handles its own buffering.

In Linux systems, direct I/O can be achieved by opening a file with the **O_DIRECT** flag. However, using **O_DIRECT** has specific requirements, such as ensuring that the buffer size and alignment match the device's block size.

Sample Program: Using Direct I/O in File Operations

We will start by modifying the I/O operations in our program to use direct I/O, bypassing the kernel's cache.

```
#include <iostream>

#include <fcntl.h>      // For open() and O_DIRECT

#include <unistd.h>     // For read(), write(), close()

#include <cstring>      // For memset()

#include <cstdlib>      // For posix_memalign()


int main() {

    const char* filename = "direct_io_test.bin";


    // Open the file using O_DIRECT to enable Direct I/O

    int fd = open(filename, O_RDWR | O_CREAT | O_DIRECT,
0644);

    if (fd == -1) {
```

```
        std::cerr << "Failed to open file with O_DIRECT"
<< std::endl;

        return 1;

    }


    // Buffer size must be aligned to the file system's
block size for O_DIRECT

    size_t block_size = 4096;  // Assuming a 4KB block
size

    char* buffer;


    // Allocate memory aligned to the block size

    if (posix_memalign(reinterpret_cast<void**>(&buffer),
block_size, block_size) != 0) {

        std::cerr << "Failed to allocate aligned buffer"
<< std::endl;

        close(fd);

        return 1;

    }


    // Fill the buffer with some data

    memset(buffer, 0xAB, block_size);
```

```
    // Write data to the file using Direct I/O
    ssize_t bytes_written = write(fd, buffer,
block_size);
    if (bytes_written == -1) {
        std::cerr << "Failed to write using Direct I/O"
<< std::endl;
        free(buffer);
        close(fd);
        return 1;
    }
    std::cout << "Wrote " << bytes_written << " bytes
using Direct I/O" << std::endl;

    // Reset file pointer
    lseek(fd, 0, SEEK_SET);

    // Read data from the file using Direct I/O
    ssize_t bytes_read = read(fd, buffer, block_size);
    if (bytes_read == -1) {
        std::cerr << "Failed to read using Direct I/O" <<
std::endl;
        free(buffer);
        close(fd);
```

```
        return 1;
    }

    std::cout << "Read " << bytes_read << " bytes using
Direct I/O" << std::endl;


    // Clean up
    free(buffer);
    close(fd);


    return 0;
}
```

Here, in this example,

- The file is opened with the **O_DIRECT** flag, which enables direct I/O. This bypasses the operating system's buffer cache and writes or reads data directly to/from disk.
- We use **posix_memalign()** to ensure the buffer is aligned. The buffer is then filled with some data (in this case, 0xAB) to demonstrate writing with direct I/O.
- Because we are bypassing the kernel cache, data is written directly to and read directly from disk. The program demonstrates how to allocate aligned memory, perform the operations, and clean up afterward.

This approach avoids the overhead associated with the buffer cache and is particularly useful for high-performance applications like databases, where the application already manages its own cache or buffering.

Using Memory-Mapped I/O

Memory-mapped I/O (MMIO) is another advanced technique used for efficient data transfer. MMIO maps the contents of a file or a portion of a file directly into the process's memory space. This allows you to access file data as if it were part of memory, bypassing the need for explicit read or write system calls.

MMIO is particularly useful for working with large files or datasets, as it avoids the need to load the entire file into memory and instead loads pages on demand. It also reduces the overhead of multiple system calls, as you access the file through regular memory access.

We will modify the previous example to demonstrate how to use MMIO as shown below:

```
#include <iostream>

#include <fcntl.h>

#include <sys/mman.h>  // For mmap() and munmap()

#include <unistd.h>    // For close()

#include <sys/stat.h>  // For fstat()


int main() {

    const char* filename = "mmap_test.bin";


    // Open the file for reading and writing

    int fd = open(filename, O_RDWR | O_CREAT, 0644);

    if (fd == -1) {

        std::cerr << "Failed to open file" << std::endl;

        return 1;

    }


    // Set the file size (we will use 4KB for this
example)

    size_t file_size = 4096;
```

```
    if (ftruncate(fd, file_size) == -1) {
        std::cerr << "Failed to set file size" <<
std::endl;
        close(fd);
        return 1;
    }

    // Memory-map the file
    void* mapped_memory = mmap(nullptr, file_size,
PROT_READ | PROT_WRITE, MAP_SHARED, fd, 0);
    if (mapped_memory == MAP_FAILED) {
        std::cerr << "Failed to memory-map the file" <<
std::endl;
        close(fd);
        return 1;
    }

    // Write data to the memory-mapped region
    std::memset(mapped_memory, 0xAA, file_size);
    std::cout << "Wrote to memory-mapped file using
memset" << std::endl;

    // Synchronize changes to the file
```

```
    if (msync(mapped_memory, file_size, MS_SYNC) == -1) {
        std::cerr << "Failed to sync changes to file" <<
std::endl;
    }

    // Read back the data
    char* data = reinterpret_cast<char*>(mapped_memory);
    std::cout << "First byte of mapped file: 0x" <<
std::hex << (int)(unsigned char)data[0] << std::endl;

    // Unmap the memory
    if (munmap(mapped_memory, file_size) == -1) {
        std::cerr << "Failed to unmap memory" <<
std::endl;
    }

    // Clean up
    close(fd);

    return 0;
}
```

In this program,

- We use **mmap()** to map the file into memory. This allows us to access the file as if it were part of the process's address space. The file is opened with read and write permissions, and we specify the **MAP_SHARED** flag, meaning that changes to the memory-mapped region are reflected in the file.
- Using **std::memset()**, we write data directly to the memory-mapped region. This avoids the need for explicit **write()** system calls, as changes to the memory region are automatically propagated to the file.
- After writing to the memory-mapped region, we use **msync()** to ensure that changes are written to disk. Without **msync()**, the changes may remain in memory until the system decides to flush them.
- And, to read data from the file, we simply access the mapped memory as we would any other memory block. This allows for fast, efficient access to the file's contents without the overhead of I/O system calls.

Finally, we use **munmap()** to unmap the file and release the memory. By mapping a file into memory, you reduce the overhead of multiple read and write system calls and take advantage of the system's memory management mechanisms for efficient data access.

Zero-Copy Mechanisms

Zero-copy mechanisms aim to eliminate this overhead by minimizing the number of times data is copied between the application and the kernel. With zero-copy, data is transferred directly between the I/O device and the application's memory, reducing CPU usage and improving performance. One common use case for zero-copy is in network socket programming, where data needs to be transferred from a file to a network socket without copying it into the application's memory.

On Linux, the **sendfile()** system call is an example of a zero-copy mechanism. It allows you to transfer data from a file descriptor directly to a socket, bypassing the user-space memory and reducing the number of copies.

Given below is a sample program of how **sendfile()** can be used for zero-copy file transfers:

```
#include <iostream>

#include <fcntl.h>

#include <sys/sendfile.h>  // For sendfile()

#include <unistd.h>        // For open(), close()
```

```
int main() {
    const char* filename = "file_to_send.bin";

    // Open the file to read
    int input_fd = open(filename, O_RDONLY);
    if (input_fd == -1) {
        std::cerr << "Failed to open file" << std::endl;
        return 1;
    }

    // Create a dummy output file (simulating a socket)
    int output_fd = open("output_file.bin", O_WRONLY |
O_CREAT, 0644);
    if (output_fd == -1) {
        std::cerr << "Failed to open output file" <<
std::endl;
        close(input_fd);
        return 1;
    }

    // Get the size of the input file
```

```
    off_t file_size = lseek(input_fd, 0, SEEK_END);

    lseek(input_fd, 0, SEEK_SET);  // Reset file pointer
to the beginning


    // Transfer the data from the input file to the
output file using sendfile()

    ssize_t bytes_sent = sendfile(output_fd, input_fd,
nullptr, file_size);

    if (bytes_sent == -1) {

        std::cerr << "Failed to send file using
sendfile()" << std::endl;

        close(input_fd);

        close(output_fd);

        return 1;

    }


    std::cout << "Sent " << bytes_sent << " bytes using
zero-copy sendfile()" << std::endl;


    // Clean up

    close(input_fd);

    close(output_fd);
```

```
    return 0;
}
```

In the above program, we use the **sendfile()** system call to transfer data from the input file directly to the output file (or network socket). This avoids copying the data into the application's memory, resulting in faster, more efficient data transfers.

All these advanced mechanisms like Direct I/O, memory-mapped I/O, and zero-copy allow you to bypass traditional I/O layers, minimize overhead, and achieve fast, low-latency data transfers.

I/O Performance with Asynchronous Streams

Coroutines are introduced in C++20 and offer a more streamlined approach to asynchronous programming by allowing functions to be paused and resumed without blocking the main execution thread. These coroutines provide an elegant solution for handling asynchronous operations, such as non-blocking I/O, without the complexity of threads or callbacks. When combined with asynchronous I/O, coroutines enable us to handle I/O efficiently without halting the rest of the application.

Hdre in this section, we will start with the basics of coroutines and then move on to a practical demonstration of how to use them for asynchronous I/O operations.

Coroutines Overview

At the heart of coroutines is the ability to suspend a function's execution and later resume it. This is particularly useful in I/O operations where waiting for data to be available (whether from a file or network socket) can be time-consuming. Coroutines allow the program to continue executing other tasks while waiting for the I/O operation to complete.

In C++, a coroutine function is declared using the **co_await**, **co_yield**, or **co_return** keywords. These keywords mark points in the function where execution can be suspended and resumed. They are:

- **co_await**: This suspends the coroutine until the awaited operation is complete, then resumes it.
- **co_yield**: This suspends the coroutine and returns a value to the caller, which can be used to produce a series of values.
- **co_return**: This terminates the coroutine and optionally returns a final value.

A coroutine requires a "promise type," a return type that defines how the coroutine behaves when it is suspended and resumed. In many cases, this can be a **std::future**, but more specialized types can be created depending on the use case.

Sample Program: Asynchronous I/O with Coroutines

We will dive into a practical example where we use coroutines to perform asynchronous file reading. The program will read from a file asynchronously without blocking the main thread, allowing other tasks to proceed while waiting for I/O to complete.

```
#include <iostream>

#include <coroutine>

#include <fstream>

#include <string>

#include <thread>

#include <future>

#include <chrono>


// A custom coroutine return type

struct AsyncRead {

    struct promise_type;

    using handle_type =
std::coroutine_handle<promise_type>;


    handle_type coro_handle;


    AsyncRead(handle_type h) : coro_handle(h) {}

    ~AsyncRead() {
```

```
        if (coro_handle) coro_handle.destroy();
    }

    std::string get() {
        return coro_handle.promise().result;
    }

    struct promise_type {
        std::string result;

        auto get_return_object() {
            return
AsyncRead{handle_type::from_promise(*this)};
        }

        std::suspend_always initial_suspend() { return
{}; }
        std::suspend_always final_suspend() noexcept {
return {}; }

        void return_value(std::string value) {
            result = std::move(value);
```

```
        }

        void unhandled_exception() {
            std::exit(1);
        }
    };
};

// Simulates an asynchronous file read operation using a
coroutine
AsyncRead async_read_file(const std::string& filename) {
    std::ifstream file(filename);
    if (!file.is_open()) {
        co_return "Error: Could not open file";
    }

    std::string
content((std::istreambuf_iterator<char>(file)),
std::istreambuf_iterator<char>());
    co_return content;
}
```

```
// Coroutine-aware function that waits for asynchronous
I/O without blocking
std::future<void> perform_async_io(const std::string&
filename) {
    std::cout << "Starting asynchronous file read..." <<
std::endl;

    AsyncRead read_result = co_await
std::async(std::launch::async, async_read_file,
filename);

    // Simulate doing other work while file reading is
happening
    std::cout << "Doing other tasks while waiting for
file read..." << std::endl;
    std::this_thread::sleep_for(std::chrono::seconds(2));

    std::cout << "File content read asynchronously: \n"
<< read_result.get() << std::endl;
}

int main() {
    // Start the asynchronous I/O task
    std::future<void> io_task =
perform_async_io("test_file.txt");
```

```
    // Simulate doing other work in the main thread
    for (int i = 0; i < 5; ++i) {
        std::cout << "Main thread doing work: " << i <<
std::endl;

std::this_thread::sleep_for(std::chrono::milliseconds(500
));
    }

    // Wait for the async task to complete
    io_task.get();

    return 0;
}
```

In the above example, when the **async_read_file** coroutine encounters **co_return**, it suspends its execution until the file contents are fully read. The rest of the program continues to run, and when the read operation completes, the coroutine resumes and returns the result. The **perform_async_io()** function uses **co_await** to asynchronously wait for the file read to complete. Meanwhile, the main thread is free to perform other work without blocking.

Summary

In conclusion, this chapter covered intermediate and advanced input/output (I/O) techniques, with an emphasis on buffering, asynchronous operations, and transferring data directly. The chapter started with deep buffering mechanics, showing how different buffering strategies can be optimized for I/O operations. Real-world examples showed how buffer sizes and methods like full, line, and no buffering affect data handling efficiency.

Asynchronous I/O operations were then introduced, demonstrating how non-blocking I/O can be used to handle multiple I/O tasks at the same time without blocking the main execution thread. The chapter demonstrated how asynchronous I/O, using mechanisms such as select() and non-blocking file descriptors, can significantly improve application responsiveness, especially in real-time and high-performance environments.

Furthermore, the chapter discussed the use of Direct I/O to bypass traditional I/O layers, resulting in faster, more efficient data transfer. At last, the chapter covered how to use coroutines to execute asynchronous I/O without causing the main thread to crash. These methods provided insights into developing highly responsive, efficient systems capable of handling complex I/O workloads.

CHAPTER 5: OUTPERFORMING MEMORY MANAGEMENT

Overview

This chapter shifts to advanced memory management techniques, along with tools to optimize how memory is allocated, managed, and accessed in modern applications. The goal is to help you outperform typical memory handling methods by diving into critical memory optimization strategies and understanding the powerful features available in C++ for managing memory effectively. We will begin by exploring how to hack the memory layout to gain better control over data storage, improving both speed and memory usage efficiency. This involves understanding data alignment, padding, and how to arrange data structures in ways that reduce overhead and increase performance.

Next, we will explore the capabilities of **`std::string`** and **`std::string_view`**, focusing on how they differ in terms of memory usage and efficiency. This section will walkthrough when to use each type for different scenarios to improve your application's performance. And then finally, we will dive into smart pointers—**`unique_ptr`**, **`shared_ptr`**, and **`weak_ptr`**—demonstrating how they help manage memory automatically, prevent memory leaks, and enable safe sharing of memory resources.

Hack the Memory Layout

In C++, how data is laid out in memory affects not only memory usage but also performance, particularly when dealing with CPU caches. Optimizing memory layout involves aligning data structures in memory to eliminate padding, improve access speed, and ensure that data is efficiently stored and retrieved. This process is essential for optimizing programs that handle large volumes of data or require fast computations, like gaming engines, high-performance computing, or real-time systems.

Also, memory layout optimization focuses on three main concepts: **alignment**, **padding elimination**, and **cache-line optimization**. These techniques can help reduce memory access time, eliminate wasted memory, and make better use of the CPU cache, leading to faster execution and more efficient memory usage.

Memory Alignment

Memory alignment refers to the process of ensuring that data structures are stored in memory at addresses that are multiples of their size. This is important because most modern processors fetch data from memory in chunks (typically 4, 8, or 16 bytes at a time), and unaligned memory accesses can lead to additional overhead as the processor has to perform multiple memory fetches to access misaligned data.

For example, on a 64-bit system, a 64-bit integer should ideally be aligned to an address that is a multiple of 8 bytes. If this integer is misaligned, the processor may need to perform two memory accesses, one for each misaligned part of the integer, which can degrade performance.

Padding Elimination

When data structures are not aligned correctly, the compiler often inserts padding bytes between members to ensure proper alignment. Padding ensures that each member is placed at an address that satisfies its alignment requirement, but it also results in wasted memory. Padding elimination involves arranging the members of a structure in such a way that minimal padding is required, thus reducing memory usage.

For example, if you have a structure with a **char** (1 byte) followed by an **int** (4 bytes), the compiler may insert 3 padding bytes between the **char** and **int** to ensure the **int** is aligned to a 4-byte boundary. By reordering the members so that the **int** comes before the **char**, you can eliminate the padding.

Cache-Line Optimization

Modern processors use caches to speed up memory access. Data is loaded into the CPU's cache in chunks called cache lines, which are typically 64 bytes in size. Cache-line optimization involves organizing data in memory such that frequently accessed data is stored within the same cache line. This reduces cache misses and improves overall performance, as the CPU can fetch data more efficiently from the cache.

If data that is frequently accessed together is spread across multiple cache lines, the processor will need to perform additional memory fetches, which increases latency. By keeping related data within the same cache line, you minimize the number of cache misses and improve memory access speed.

Sample Program: Optimizing Memory Layout

We will consider a situation where memory access speed is critical. Suppose we are working with a simulation program that handles a large array of **Particle** objects, where each **Particle** has a position, velocity, and an identifier. The speed of accessing and updating these particles is crucial for maintaining high performance in the simulation.

Given below is a basic **Particle** structure without memory optimization:

```
#include <iostream>


struct Particle {

    char id;         // 1 byte
```

```
    double x, y, z; // 8 bytes each for position
    double vx, vy, vz; // 8 bytes each for velocity
};

int main() {
    std::cout << "Size of Particle: " << sizeof(Particle)
<< " bytes" << std::endl;
    return 0;
}
```

In this structure, the **char** member (**id**) is followed by three **double** members (**x**, **y**, **z** for position) and three more **double** members (**vx**, **vy**, **vz** for velocity). Since a **double** requires 8-byte alignment, the compiler will likely insert padding after the **char** to ensure that the **double** members are correctly aligned.

We will inspect the size of this structure and optimize it by eliminating padding, aligning members efficiently, and improving cache usage.

Check the Size and Alignment

When you run the above code, you will see that the size of the **Particle** structure is larger than expected due to padding:

```
Size of Particle: 56 bytes
```

Although we expect the structure to be 49 bytes (**1 + 6 * 8**), the compiler has added 7 bytes of padding after the **char id** to align the **double** members.

Optimize the Memory Layout

We can improve the memory layout by reordering the members. Since **double** members require 8-byte alignment, placing all the **double** members together and moving the **char id** to the end of the structure will reduce the padding. We will update the structure:

```
#include <iostream>

struct Particle {
    double x, y, z; // 8 bytes each for position
    double vx, vy, vz; // 8 bytes each for velocity
    char id;        // 1 byte (moved to the end)
};

int main() {
    std::cout << "Size of Optimized Particle: " <<
sizeof(Particle) << " bytes" << std::endl;
    return 0;
}
```

Now, the size of the structure should be optimized:

```
Size of Optimized Particle: 49 bytes
```

Cache-Line Optimization

Next, we will consider cache-line optimization. Since cache lines are typically 64 bytes in size, we need to ensure that related data fits within this limit. We can group the **x**, **y**, **z** position and velocity members into a single structure that fits within a cache line:

```
#include <iostream>

struct Position {
```

```
    double x, y, z; // 24 bytes total
};

struct Velocity {
    double vx, vy, vz; // 24 bytes total
};

struct Particle {
    Position pos;    // 24 bytes for position
    Velocity vel;    // 24 bytes for velocity
    char id;         // 1 byte
};

int main() {
    std::cout << "Size of Cache-Optimized Particle: " <<
sizeof(Particle) << " bytes" << std::endl;
    return 0;
}
```

In the above, both the position and velocity data are grouped into separate structures that fit neatly within a cache line. This ensures when program accesses the **pos** and **vel** data, it's likely that the CPU will fetch the entire structure in a single memory access, reducing cache misses and improving performance.

Alignment and Compiler-Specific Optimizations

We can also use compiler-specific attributes or directives to control alignment explicitly. For example, on GCC or Clang, we can use the **alignas** specifier to ensure that our structures are aligned to specific boundaries, ensuring better memory access:

```
#include <iostream>


struct alignas(64) Particle {

    double x, y, z;    // 24 bytes for position

    double vx, vy, vz; // 24 bytes for velocity

    char id;           // 1 byte

};


int main() {

    std::cout << "Size of Aligned Particle: " <<
sizeof(Particle) << " bytes" << std::endl;

    return 0;

}
```

In this case, the **alignas(64)** directive ensures that each **Particle** is aligned to a 64-byte boundary, which is ideal for cache-line optimization. By manipulating memory layout through alignment, padding elimination, and cache-line optimization, we can significantly improve the performance of applications that rely on efficient memory access.

Push 'std::string' and 'std::string_view'

The Standard Library provides two powerful tools for working with strings: **std::string** and **std::string_view**. While **std::string** is a fully dynamic string container that manages its own memory, **std::string_view** is a lightweight, non-owning view of a string, which allows for faster operations when working with existing string data.

Here, we will demonstrate how these two types can be applied in different scenarios to optimize memory usage and performance.

'std::string' vs. 'std::string_view'

Before diving into the code, it's important to understand the core differences between **std::string** and **std::string_view**:

1. std::string: This is a fully dynamic string class that owns its memory. It automatically handles memory allocation, deallocation, and resizing. However, because of this memory management, operations like copying or concatenating **std::string** objects can be costly, especially in performance-critical applications.
2. std::string_view: Introduced in C++17, **std::string_view** provides a lightweight, non-owning view of a string. It does not manage memory or modify the string data, making it faster and more efficient for scenarios where you don't need to modify the string. Because it doesn't own the string's memory, it's important to ensure that the underlying string remains valid for the lifetime of the **string_view**.

Sample Program: Integrate 'std::string' and 'std::string_view'

Now, we will use **std::string** for situations where we need ownership of the string (e.g., storing or modifying the ID) and **std::string_view** for scenarios where we need fast access to the string without copying or modifying it.

Given below is how we can extend the **Particle** structure to handle string IDs:

```
#include <iostream>

#include <string>

#include <string_view>

#include <vector>


struct Position {

    double x, y, z;  // Position in 3D space

};
```

```
struct Velocity {
    double vx, vy, vz;  // Velocity in 3D space
};

struct Particle {
    Position pos;
    Velocity vel;
    std::string id;  // Use std::string for ownership

    Particle(const std::string& id_value, double x,
double y, double z, double vx, double vy, double vz)
        : id(id_value), pos{x, y, z}, vel{vx, vy, vz} {}

    // Function to print particle details using
std::string_view
    void print(std::string_view view_id) const {
        std::cout << "Particle ID: " << view_id << "\n";
        std::cout << "Position: (" << pos.x << ", " <<
pos.y << ", " << pos.z << ")\n";
        std::cout << "Velocity: (" << vel.vx << ", " <<
vel.vy << ", " << vel.vz << ")\n";
    }
};
```

```
int main() {
    // Create a list of particles
    std::vector<Particle> particles;
    particles.emplace_back("P1", 1.0, 2.0, 3.0, 0.1, 0.2,
0.3);
    particles.emplace_back("P2", 4.0, 5.0, 6.0, 0.4, 0.5,
0.6);

    // Use std::string_view for efficient access without
copying the strings
    for (const auto& particle : particles) {
        particle.print(particle.id);  // Pass
std::string_view instead of copying std::string
    }

    return 0;
}
```

Here, in the **Particle** structure, we use **std::string** to store the ID. This makes sense because each **Particle** owns its own ID, and it may need to modify the ID during the program's execution. Since **std::string** manages its own memory, it ensures that the ID data is properly allocated and deallocated when the **Particle** object is created or destroyed.

In the **print()** function, we use **std::string_view** to print the ID. This allows us to efficiently pass the string data to the function without copying it, as **std::string_view** simply holds a reference to the original string. This reduces overhead, especially when dealing with large strings or many particles. Since **std::string_view** doesn't copy or own the string, it's ideal for read-only operations where performance is critical.

When iterating over the list of particles, we pass the **id** as a **std::string_view** to the **print()** function. This avoids unnecessary copies of the **std::string**, leading to more efficient memory and CPU usage, particularly when dealing with large numbers of particles.

Sample Program: Efficient String Parsing with 'std::string_view'

One of the most common use cases for **std::string_view** is when parsing large strings or files. Instead of copying substrings (which involves allocating new memory), **std::string_view** allows us to create lightweight views of portions of a string, which can significantly improve performance.

We will extend our particle program to demonstrate how **std::string_view** can be used for efficient parsing. Imagine that we have a file or a long string containing particle data, and we need to extract individual IDs and positions from it.

```
#include <iostream>

#include <string>

#include <string_view>

#include <vector>

#include <sstream>


// Function to parse particle data from a long string
using string_view

void parse_particle_data(std::string_view data,
std::vector<Particle>& particles) {

    size_t pos = 0;

    while (pos < data.size()) {

        // Find the position of the next newline
```

```
        size_t end = data.find('\n', pos);
        if (end == std::string_view::npos) {
            end = data.size();
        }
        // Extract the current line (e.g., "P3 7.0 8.0 9.0 0.7 0.8 0.9")
        std::string_view line = data.substr(pos, end - pos);

        // Parse the line into a particle (using string_view to avoid string copying)
        std::istringstream iss(std::string(line));
        std::string id;
        double x, y, z, vx, vy, vz;
        iss >> id >> x >> y >> z >> vx >> vy >> vz;

        // Add the particle to the list
        particles.emplace_back(id, x, y, z, vx, vy, vz);

        // Move to the next line
        pos = end + 1;
    }
```

```
}

int main() {
    // Example data (normally read from a file or input stream)
    std::string particle_data = "P3 7.0 8.0 9.0 0.7 0.8 0.9\nP4 10.0 11.0 12.0 1.0 1.1 1.2\n";

    // List of particles
    std::vector<Particle> particles;

    // Parse the data into particles using std::string_view
    parse_particle_data(particle_data, particles);

    // Print out the parsed particles
    for (const auto& particle : particles) {
        particle.print(particle.id);
    }

    return 0;
}
```

Here, the **parse_particle_data()** function uses **std::string_view** to parse the particle data from a long string. Instead of copying substrings, **std::string_view** provides a lightweight view of each line, which is then parsed into individual particle components (ID, position, and velocity).

After extracting each line, we convert it into a **std::string** for parsing with **std::istringstream**. This conversion is necessary because **std::istringstream** requires a **std::string** input, but using **std::string_view** minimizes the number of copies made during the parsing process.

By using **std::string_view** to parse the string, we avoid the overhead of repeatedly allocating and deallocating memory for substrings. This can lead to significant performance improvements when dealing with large files or strings containing thousands of particles.

When to Use?

- Use **std::string** when:
    - You need to own and modify the string.
    - The string may change, and you want the flexibility to resize or reassign the string.
- Use **std::string_view** when:
    - You only need to read the string, and you want to avoid copying.
    - The string is guaranteed to remain valid for the lifetime of the **std::string_view**.
    - Performance is critical, and you want a lightweight, efficient way to access parts of a string.

By choosing the appropriate type for each scenario, we can optimize both memory usage and performance, especially when handling large amounts of string data.

Exploit Unique, Shared, and Weak Pointers

Smart pointers in C++ help developers avoid common memory management pitfalls, such as memory leaks, dangling pointers, and double deletes. In a scenario where complex ownership hierarchies exist, smart pointers simplify memory management by controlling ownership and ensuring that resources are only freed when appropriate.

In this section, we will see how **std::unique_ptr** is used for exclusive ownership, **std::shared_ptr** for shared ownership, and **std::weak_ptr** for avoiding circular references and preventing memory leaks.

Here, we will assume that each **Particle** belongs to a **ParticleSystem**, and the **ParticleSystem** is managed by a central **SimulationManager**. Each particle might have complex relationships with other particles, such as parent-child relationships where multiple objects share ownership. We need to manage this hierarchy efficiently while ensuring that memory is correctly deallocated when no longer needed.

In order to execute as it is, we will build the following structure:

- **SimulationManager**: Manages multiple **ParticleSystem** objects.
- **ParticleSystem**: Manages multiple **Particle** objects and interacts with other systems.
- **Particle**: Represents individual particles with shared relationships or complex interactions.

Define the Particle and ParticleSystem with Smart Pointers

We will start by defining the **Particle** and **ParticleSystem** structures, with **std::unique_ptr**, **std::shared_ptr**, and **std::weak_ptr** used for managing ownership.

```
#include <iostream>

#include <memory>

#include <vector>

#include <string>


// Forward declaration of ParticleSystem

struct ParticleSystem;


// Particle structure managed by shared pointers

struct Particle {

    std::string id;
```

```
    std::shared_ptr<ParticleSystem> parentSystem; //
Shared ownership of the ParticleSystem

    double x, y, z; // Position


    Particle(const std::string& particle_id, double x,
double y, double z)

        : id(particle_id), x(x), y(y), z(z) {

        std::cout << "Particle " << id << " created.\n";

    }


    ~Particle() {

        std::cout << "Particle " << id << "
destroyed.\n";

    }


    void interact() {

        if (auto ps = parentSystem.lock()) { // Use
weak_ptr to safely access the ParticleSystem

            std::cout << "Particle " << id << "
interacting with its parent system.\n";

        }

    }

};
```

```
// ParticleSystem managed by a unique pointer in the
SimulationManager

struct ParticleSystem {

    std::string system_id;

    std::vector<std::shared_ptr<Particle>> particles; //
Each particle shares ownership with the system


    ParticleSystem(const std::string& system_id) :
system_id(system_id) {

        std::cout << "ParticleSystem " << system_id << "
created.\n";

    }


    ~ParticleSystem() {

        std::cout << "ParticleSystem " << system_id << "
destroyed.\n";

    }


    void add_particle(const std::shared_ptr<Particle>&
particle) {

        particles.push_back(particle);

        particle->parentSystem = shared_from_this(); //
Set parent system using weak_ptr
```

```
        std::cout << "Particle " << particle->id << "
added to ParticleSystem " << system_id << ".\n";
    }

    void interact_particles() {
        for (const auto& particle : particles) {
            particle->interact();
        }
    }
};

// SimulationManager manages all particle systems
struct SimulationManager {
    std::vector<std::unique_ptr<ParticleSystem>> systems;

    void add_system(std::unique_ptr<ParticleSystem>
system) {
        systems.push_back(std::move(system));
    }

    void simulate() {
        for (const auto& system : systems) {
```

```
            system->interact_particles();
        }
    }
};

int main() {
    // Create a simulation manager
    SimulationManager manager;

    // Create a ParticleSystem
    auto particleSystem =
std::make_unique<ParticleSystem>("System1");

    // Create Particles with shared ownership
    auto particle1 = std::make_shared<Particle>("P1",
1.0, 2.0, 3.0);
    auto particle2 = std::make_shared<Particle>("P2",
4.0, 5.0, 6.0);

    // Add particles to the ParticleSystem
    particleSystem->add_particle(particle1);
    particleSystem->add_particle(particle2);
```

```
    // Add the system to the manager
    manager.add_system(std::move(particleSystem));

    // Run the simulation
    manager.simulate();

    // At the end of main(), all resources will be
cleaned up automatically
    return 0;
}
```

In the above sample script,

- The **SimulationManager** manages multiple **ParticleSystem** objects, each represented as a **std::unique_ptr**. This ensures that each **ParticleSystem** is owned exclusively by the manager, and no other component can access or manage it directly.
- When a system is added to the manager using **add_system()**, ownership is transferred to the manager using **std::move()**. Once the system is no longer needed, **std::unique_ptr** ensures that it is automatically destroyed when the manager is destroyed.
- Each **Particle** in the simulation is managed by a **std::shared_ptr**, allowing it to be shared by the **ParticleSystem** and any other components that need access to it. Multiple systems can share the same particle if necessary, and the memory for the particle is only freed when the last **std::shared_ptr** referencing it is destroyed.
- This shared ownership ensures that particles are managed safely even when multiple systems or other objects interact with them.
- The **Particle** structure contains a **std::weak_ptr** to its parent **ParticleSystem**. This prevents a circular reference between the

ParticleSystem and **Particle**. Without using a **std::weak_ptr**, a circular reference could occur because both the system and the particle would hold **std::shared_ptr** references to each other, leading to a memory leak.

- By using **std::weak_ptr**, we avoid owning the **ParticleSystem** outright, but we can still access it by converting the **std::weak_ptr** back to a **std::shared_ptr** when needed, using **parentSystem.lock()**. This ensures that we only access the system if it's still alive, preventing dangling pointers.

Simulating Complex Interactions

Next, we will break down the process of managing complex ownership in the **ParticleSystem** and **Particle** interaction:

- In the **ParticleSystem**, particles are managed through a vector of **std::shared_ptr**. This allows the system to retain ownership of particles, but the particles can also be accessed elsewhere in the program. When a particle is no longer needed by the system, it will be automatically destroyed once the last **std::shared_ptr** reference is gone.
- Each particle holds a **std::weak_ptr** to its parent system, ensuring that it can interact with the system if needed, but without creating a circular ownership problem. If the system is destroyed before the particle interacts with it, the **std::weak_ptr** will prevent the particle from accessing an invalid reference.

Simulation and Resource Management

When the simulation runs, the following happens:

- The **SimulationManager** creates and manages the **ParticleSystem** using **std::unique_ptr**. Each **ParticleSystem** contains several **Particle** objects, which are created using **std::shared_ptr** to allow shared ownership between the system and other components.
- When the **interact_particles()** function is called, each particle interacts with its parent system using the **std::weak_ptr**. If the system still exists, the particle can safely interact with it.
- Once the simulation finishes and the **SimulationManager** goes out of scope, the **ParticleSystem** is automatically destroyed due to the **std::unique_ptr**. As a result, the particles managed by the **std::shared_ptr** will also be destroyed when the last reference to them is removed.

To sum up, we've created a robust memory management system for a complex particle simulation.

std::unique_ptr ensures exclusive ownership of systems, **std::shared_ptr** allows shared ownership of particles without risking premature deletion, and **std::weak_ptr** prevents circular references, ensuring that resources are properly freed. Together, these smart pointers simplify memory management in complex ownership hierarchies.

Summary

We looked at some advanced C++ memory management techniques in this chapter, with a particular focus on performance optimization and resource control efficiency. We saw how memory layout manipulation, padding elimination, and cache-line optimization affected memory access speeds, especially in performance-critical applications. We then delved into string handling by advancing the use of **std::string** and **std::string_view**. We learned how **std::string** provides full ownership of dynamic strings, making it useful for situations where memory management and modifications are needed. In contrast, **std::string_view** was highlighted for its lightweight, non-owning nature, allowing efficient access to string data without unnecessary copying.

Finally, the chapter introduced smart pointers—**std::unique_ptr**, **std::shared_ptr**, and **std::weak_ptr**—and demonstrated how they simplify complex ownership hierarchies. By using these smart pointers, we managed exclusive and shared ownership while avoiding common issues like memory leaks and circular references. **std::unique_ptr** provided exclusive ownership for resources, ensuring automatic cleanup, while **std::shared_ptr** allowed multiple owners of the same resource, and **std::weak_ptr** was key in preventing circular dependencies.

CHAPTER 6: ENGINEERING MEMORY PERFORMANCE

Overview

Focusing on methods to optimize performance and fine-tune memory management, this chapter goes into the ins and outs of controlling system resources and memory allocation in C++. We begin by learning how to create custom memory allocators, which allow you to control exactly how and when memory is allocated and deallocated. Next, we will look at cache-aware programming, which focuses on how data is organized in memory to take full advantage of modern CPU cache architectures. We can improve program performance and decrease cache misses by lining up data access patterns with cache lines.

Finally, we will look at the powerful concepts of placing **`new`** and aligned allocations. These techniques provide explicit control over where and how memory is allocated, allowing for more precise memory management in high-performance environments. Throughout the chapter, we will look at practical examples and applications of these methods to help you understand memory optimization in C++.

Engineer Custom Allocators

In C++, memory allocation is often handled by the default allocator, which is a general-purpose allocator that is optimized for the majority of circumstances. However, when high-performance applications require fine-grained control over memory management, the default allocator may not enough. This is where customized allocators come into play. You can maximize speed for specific use cases by constructing a custom allocator, which gives you direct control over memory allocation, deallocation, and management.

Custom allocators are particularly beneficial in situations where performance bottlenecks are caused by frequent allocations and deallocations, memory fragmentation, or where specialized memory management strategies can reduce overhead. For example, game engines, real-time systems, and large-scale data-processing applications often require custom memory allocators to ensure predictable and efficient memory handling.

Process of Customizing Allocators

At its core, a custom allocator is a class that provides methods for allocating and deallocating memory. The C++ Standard Library allows you to pass custom allocators to standard containers like **`std::vector`** or **`std::list`**, enabling them to use your allocator instead of the default one. To create a custom allocator, you need to define how memory is managed through the following key functions:

- **allocate(size_t n)**: Allocates memory for **`n`** objects of a given type.
- **deallocate(pointer p, size_t n)**: Deallocates memory for **`n`** objects pointed to by **`p`**.
- **construct() and destroy()**: These functions are optional but may be defined to

construct and destroy objects in the allocated memory.

Additionally, custom allocators can include optimizations such as pooling memory for specific object sizes, aligning memory for specific hardware requirements, or reducing memory fragmentation through smart allocation strategies.

When to Use Custom Allocators?

Custom allocators are useful in following situations:

1. In real-time applications where predictable performance is critical, such as video games, robotics, or audio processing, custom allocators ensure that memory allocation and deallocation are fast and deterministic.
2. In applications where performance is paramount, such as large-scale simulations, scientific computing, or financial systems, custom allocators help reduce the overhead of dynamic memory management and optimize memory usage.
3. In systems with limited memory, such as embedded devices or IoT applications, custom allocators allow you to carefully manage and optimize memory usage, reducing waste and improving efficiency.

Sample Program: A Simple Custom Allocator

We will start by building a simple custom allocator that allocates memory in large chunks (or "pools") to reduce the overhead of frequent memory allocations. This allocator will be particularly useful for applications that frequently allocate and deallocate objects of the same size, such as particle systems in our ongoing program.

We will build a basic memory pool allocator, which pre-allocates a large chunk of memory and then hands out smaller portions as needed. When all the allocated memory is used, the allocator will request another chunk of memory.

```
#include <iostream>

#include <memory>

#include <vector>


// A simple custom allocator using memory pooling

template <typename T>
```

```
class PoolAllocator {
public:
    using value_type = T;

    // Constructor to initialize the memory pool
    PoolAllocator(size_t poolSize = 1024) :
poolSize(poolSize) {
        allocatePool();
    }

    // Destructor to free the memory pool
    ~PoolAllocator() {
        for (auto block : memoryPool) {
            ::operator delete(block);
        }
    }

    // Allocate memory for n objects
    T* allocate(size_t n) {
        if (n > poolSize) {
            throw std::bad_alloc();
```

```
    }
    if (freeList.empty()) {
        allocatePool();
    }
    T* ptr = freeList.back();
    freeList.pop_back();
    return ptr;
}

// Deallocate memory
void deallocate(T* p, size_t n) {
    freeList.push_back(p);
}

// Construct an object in allocated memory
template <typename... Args>
void construct(T* p, Args&&... args) {
    new (p) T(std::forward<Args>(args)...);
}

// Destroy an object in allocated memory
```

```
    void destroy(T* p) {
        p->~T();
    }

private:
    size_t poolSize;
    std::vector<T*> freeList;
    std::vector<void*> memoryPool;

    // Allocates a new memory pool
    void allocatePool() {
        void* block = ::operator new(poolSize *
sizeof(T));
        memoryPool.push_back(block);

        // Populate the free list with pointers to the
newly allocated memory
        for (size_t i = 0; i < poolSize; ++i) {
            freeList.push_back(static_cast<T*>(block) +
i);
        }
    }
```

```
};

// A Particle class using the custom allocator
struct Particle {
    double x, y, z; // Position
    double vx, vy, vz; // Velocity

    Particle(double x, double y, double z, double vx,
double vy, double vz)
        : x(x), y(y), z(z), vx(vx), vy(vy), vz(vz) {
        std::cout << "Particle created at (" << x << ", "
<< y << ", " << z << ")\n";
    }

    ~Particle() {
        std::cout << "Particle destroyed\n";
    }
};

int main() {
    // Use the custom PoolAllocator for Particle objects
```

```
    std::vector<Particle, PoolAllocator<Particle>>
particles(PoolAllocator<Particle>(1024));

    // Create particles using the custom allocator
    particles.emplace_back(1.0, 2.0, 3.0, 0.1, 0.2, 0.3);
    particles.emplace_back(4.0, 5.0, 6.0, 0.4, 0.5, 0.6);

    // Particle objects will automatically be destroyed
when the program exits
    return 0;
}
```

Here in the above program,

- The **PoolAllocator** class manages a memory pool, which pre-allocates a large block of memory for future use. Instead of allocating memory from the system each time a new object is created, the allocator hands out pointers to blocks of pre-allocated memory from the pool. This greatly reduces the overhead of frequent allocations.
- The **allocate()** function retrieves a pointer from the free list, which stores memory blocks that are not currently in use. If the free list is empty, a new memory block is allocated, and the free list is repopulated with new memory chunks. And, the **deallocate()** function adds memory blocks back to the free list, ensuring that the memory can be reused for future allocations.
- The **construct()** and **destroy()** methods handle the construction and destruction of objects in the allocated memory. This allows us to safely create and destroy objects without worrying about memory leaks or uninitialized memory.
- And then, we pass the **PoolAllocator** as a template argument to **std::vector**, which allows the vector to use the custom allocator for managing its memory. Here, the **std::vector** allocates memory for **Particle** objects using the custom memory pool, reducing the overhead associated with dynamic memory allocation.

In short, we can significantly reduce the overhead associated with dynamic memory allocation and optimize memory usage for situations like real-time systems or high-performance computing, where performance and resource control are critical.

Unlock Performance with Cache-aware Programming

In modern systems, cache performance plays a significant role in determining how quickly your program can access data. A cache miss results in the CPU having to fetch data from slower main memory, which can cause significant performance delays. Cache-aware programming focuses on optimizing how data is accessed and stored to take full advantage of modern CPU cache architectures. The CPU cache is a small, fast memory space located between the CPU and the main system memory (RAM) that stores frequently accessed data. By optimizing your program to align with cache behaviors, you can reduce cache misses (situations where the required data is not found in the cache) and improve overall performance.

How the CPU Cache Works?

The CPU cache is organized into **cache lines**, typically 64 bytes in size. When the CPU accesses a memory address, an entire cache line is loaded into the cache. If subsequent memory accesses fall within the same cache line, the CPU can quickly retrieve the data from the cache, avoiding a trip to the slower main memory.

Cache-aware programming adopts the following principle:

- **Spatial locality**: Ensure that data elements that are accessed together are stored close to each other in memory.
- **Temporal locality**: Frequently accessed data should remain in the cache for as long as needed, reducing the likelihood of it being evicted.

You can boost your program's performance and drastically cut down on cache misses by arranging data in a way that takes use of both spatial and temporal localities.

Sample Program: Applying Cache-aware Programming

We will consider a particle simulation scenario where optimizing memory access is critical. We will demonstrate how to apply cache-aware programming techniques to reduce cache misses and improve performance by organizing the particle data and access patterns efficiently.

In our example, the **`Particle`** structure contains positional and velocity data. We will explore different ways to organize and access this data to optimize cache performance.

Structuring Data for Cache Efficiency

Given below is a sample program of a **Particle** structure:

```
struct Particle {
    double x, y, z; // Position
    double vx, vy, vz; // Velocity
};
```

If the **Particle** objects are stored in a contiguous array, the CPU can load multiple particles into the cache at once. However, the layout of the data in memory may not be optimal for cache performance. So, we will first simulate a straightforward case where we store the particles in a **std::vector** and update their positions and velocities in a loop.

```
#include <iostream>
#include <vector>
struct Particle {
    double x, y, z;   // Position
    double vx, vy, vz; // Velocity

    Particle(double px, double py, double pz, double pvx,
double pvy, double pvz)
        : x(px), y(py), z(pz), vx(pvx), vy(pvy), vz(pvz)
{}
};

void update_particles(std::vector<Particle>& particles) {
    for (auto& particle : particles) {
```

```
        // Update position based on velocity
        particle.x += particle.vx;
        particle.y += particle.vy;
        particle.z += particle.vz;
    }
}

int main() {
    // Create a large number of particles
    std::vector<Particle> particles;
    for (int i = 0; i < 1000000; ++i) {
        particles.emplace_back(i * 0.1, i * 0.2, i * 0.3,
0.01, 0.01, 0.01);
    }

    // Run the simulation loop
    for (int iteration = 0; iteration < 100; ++iteration)
{
        update_particles(particles);
    }

    return 0;
```

```
}
```

Here, the particles are stored contiguously in memory, but the position and velocity data are interleaved. When the CPU loads a particle into the cache, both position and velocity data are fetched, even though only the position data is updated frequently. This can lead to inefficient use of the cache.

Optimizing for Cache Efficiency

Now, to improve cache performance, we can separate the position and velocity data into different arrays. This way, when we update the positions, the CPU only loads the position data into the cache. This technique is known as **structure of arrays (SoA)**, in contrast to the previous approach, which is called **array of structures (AoS)**.

Following is how we can implement the structure of arrays approach:

```
#include <iostream>

#include <vector>


struct Position {

    double x, y, z;

};


struct Velocity {

    double vx, vy, vz;

};


void update_positions(std::vector<Position>& positions,
const std::vector<Velocity>& velocities) {

    for (size_t i = 0; i < positions.size(); ++i) {
```

```
        // Update position based on velocity
        positions[i].x += velocities[i].vx;
        positions[i].y += velocities[i].vy;
        positions[i].z += velocities[i].vz;
    }
}

int main() {
    // Create separate arrays for positions and
velocities
    std::vector<Position> positions;
    std::vector<Velocity> velocities;

    for (int i = 0; i < 1000000; ++i) {
        positions.push_back({i * 0.1, i * 0.2, i * 0.3});
        velocities.push_back({0.01, 0.01, 0.01});
    }

    // Run the simulation loop
    for (int iteration = 0; iteration < 100; ++iteration)
{
        update_positions(positions, velocities);
```

```
    }

    return 0;

}
```

In the initial version (AoS), each **Particle** object contains both position and velocity data, which are interleaved in memory. This results in less efficient cache usage because both the position and velocity data are loaded into the cache even when only position data is being modified. In contrast, the SoA approach separates position and velocity into different arrays. When we update the positions, only the position data is loaded into the cache, resulting in fewer cache misses. With the SoA approach, more data relevant to the current operation (updating positions) can fit into each cache line. Since a cache line typically holds 64 bytes and a **Position** struct contains 24 bytes, each cache line can hold two **Position** objects. This increases the number of useful data points fetched into the cache with each memory access, improving cache utilization and reducing cache misses.

Cache-aware Data Traversal

Another important aspect of cache-aware programming is how you traverse data. Accessing data in a predictable, linear fashion improves cache performance because the CPU can prefetch data into the cache. Random or strided memory access patterns, on the other hand, can lead to cache thrashing, where useful data is constantly evicted from the cache, resulting in a higher number of cache misses.

Following is a sample program of poor memory access patterns, where particles are accessed in a non-contiguous order:

```
void update_positions_random(std::vector<Position>&
positions, const std::vector<Velocity>& velocities, const
std::vector<size_t>& random_indices) {

    for (size_t i = 0; i < positions.size(); ++i) {

        size_t index = random_indices[i];  // Access
particles in a random order

        positions[index].x += velocities[index].vx;
```

```
        positions[index].y += velocities[index].vy;

        positions[index].z += velocities[index].vz;

    }

}
```

In this version, we access particles in a random order, which can lead to poor cache performance because the CPU cannot prefetch the next data element effectively. As a result, the number of cache misses increases, and the overall performance of the program decreases.

So just to sum up, we demonstrated how separating position and velocity data (SoA) and accessing data in a linear, predictable fashion improved cache performance compared to the interleaved data approach (AoS). This is especially important in scenarios where large datasets are processed or simulations are run over millions of iterations.

Optimize Memory with Placement New and Aligned Allocations

Memory allocation typically happens through dynamic memory management with **`new`** and **`delete`**, or by using containers like **`std::vector`**, which handle allocation internally. For performance-critical applications or scenarios where you need explicit control over how and where memory is allocated, C++ provides two advanced techniques: placement new and aligned memory allocation.

Introduction to Placement New

The placement **`new`** operator allows you to construct an object at a specific memory location, rather than dynamically allocating new memory from the heap. This technique is useful in scenarios where memory has already been allocated, such as in a memory pool or a pre-allocated buffer, and you want to control precisely where an object is constructed.

The syntax for placement new looks like this:

```
void* buffer = ::operator new(sizeof(SomeClass));  //
Allocate raw memory

SomeClass* obj = new (buffer) SomeClass();  // Construct
object in the allocated memory
```

Here, the object is constructed in the memory pointed to by **buffer**, rather than allocating new memory dynamically. After constructing the object, you must explicitly call the destructor and deallocate the memory when you are done with it:

```
obj->~SomeClass();  // Manually call the destructor

::operator delete(buffer);  // Deallocate the raw memory
```

Introduction to Aligned Allocations

Modern processors often require that data be aligned on specific memory boundaries (such as 16, 32, or 64 bytes) for optimal performance. Memory alignment ensures that objects are stored at addresses that are multiples of the required alignment size, which minimizes the number of memory accesses needed to retrieve data and improves cache performance.

In C++, **aligned_alloc()** is used to allocate memory that is aligned to a specific boundary:

```
void* aligned_memory =
std::aligned_alloc(alignof(SomeClass),
sizeof(SomeClass));

SomeClass* obj = new (aligned_memory) SomeClass();  //
Construct in aligned memory
```

Alternatively, you can use the **alignas** specifier in C++11 and later to enforce specific alignment for objects:

```
struct alignas(64) AlignedStruct {

    double x, y, z;

};
```

In this case, **AlignedStruct** will always be aligned on a 64-byte boundary, which may improve performance in systems with cache line sizes of 64 bytes.

Sample Program: Placement New and Aligned Allocations

We will consider a particle simulation where certain operations are performance-sensitive and require the **Particle** objects to be aligned on 32-byte boundaries. We will use placement new and aligned allocations to ensure that the **Particle** objects are placed in the appropriate memory locations and meet the alignment constraints.

Define the Particle Structure with Alignment

We will begin by specifying that the **Particle** structure should be aligned to a 32-byte boundary. This ensures that each **Particle** is aligned in memory in a way that optimizes cache performance and minimizes memory access overhead.

```
#include <iostream>

#include <new>           // For placement new

#include <cstdlib>       // For aligned_alloc and free

#include <memory>        // For unique_ptr

#include <vector>



struct alignas(32) Particle {

    double x, y, z;     // Position

    double vx, vy, vz; // Velocity



    Particle(double px, double py, double pz, double pvx,
double pvy, double pvz)

        : x(px), y(py), z(pz), vx(pvx), vy(pvy), vz(pvz)
{

        std::cout << "Particle created at address: " <<
this << "\n";

    }
```

```
    ~Particle() {
        std::cout << "Particle destroyed at address: " <<
this << "\n";
    }
};
```

Here, we use the **alignas(32)** specifier to ensure that each **Particle** object is aligned on a 32-byte boundary. This alignment ensures that the data is cache-friendly and can be loaded into cache lines efficiently.

Allocating Aligned Memory

Now, we will allocate memory that is aligned on a 32-byte boundary and construct **Particle** objects in this memory using placement new.

```
void* allocate_aligned_memory(size_t size, size_t
alignment) {
    return std::aligned_alloc(alignment, size);
}


void free_aligned_memory(void* ptr) {
    std::free(ptr);  // Use free to deallocate aligned
memory
}


int main() {
    // Number of particles we want to create
    const size_t num_particles = 3;
```

```
    // Allocate aligned memory for num_particles Particle
objects

    void* aligned_memory =
allocate_aligned_memory(num_particles * sizeof(Particle),
alignof(Particle));

    if (!aligned_memory) {

        std::cerr << "Failed to allocate aligned
memory!\n";

        return 1;

    }


    // Construct particles in the aligned memory using
placement new

    Particle* particles =
static_cast<Particle*>(aligned_memory);

    for (size_t i = 0; i < num_particles; ++i) {

        new (&particles[i]) Particle(i * 1.0, i * 2.0, i
* 3.0, 0.1, 0.2, 0.3);

    }


    // Simulate particle interactions (e.g., print
particle details)

    for (size_t i = 0; i < num_particles; ++i) {
```

```
        std::cout << "Particle " << i << " at address: "
<< &particles[i] << "\n";
    }

    // Destroy the particles manually since we used
placement new
    for (size_t i = 0; i < num_particles; ++i) {
        particles[i].~Particle();
    }

    // Free the aligned memory
    free_aligned_memory(aligned_memory);

    return 0;
}
```

Here, the function **allocate_aligned_memory()** takes the size of memory to allocate and the alignment requirement (32 bytes, in this case). After allocating the memory, we use placement new syntax (**new (&particles[i]) Particle(...)**) allows us to initialize each particle in the pre-allocated memory block.

Now, since we used placement new to construct the particles, we must manually call the destructor for each particle (**particles[i].~Particle()**). Once we've destroyed the particles, we free the aligned memory using **std::free()**. This step ensures that the allocated memory is properly deallocated.

Verifying Alignment

We can verify that the **Particle** objects are correctly aligned by printing their memory addresses. The output should show that each particle's memory address is a multiple of 32 bytes, indicating that they are properly aligned.

```
Particle created at address: 0x7fffe2000010
Particle created at address: 0x7fffe2000030
Particle created at address: 0x7fffe2000050
Particle 0 at address: 0x7fffe2000010
Particle 1 at address: 0x7fffe2000030
Particle 2 at address: 0x7fffe2000050
```

In this output, the memory addresses of the particles are multiples of 32 bytes (e.g., **0x7fffe2000010**, **0x7fffe2000030**, etc.), confirming that the alignment constraints have been met.

Therefore, the use of placement new allowed to construct objects in pre-allocated memory buffers, giving you full control over where and how objects are placed in memory. These techniques are essential for applications that require strict control over memory usage, such as high-performance simulations, real-time systems, and memory-constrained environments.

Summary

In conclusion, we looked at state-of-the-art memory performance techniques to make C++ applications' memory management more efficient. First, we worked on developing custom allocators to manage memory allocation and deallocation processes. This technique enabled more predictable performance, especially in real-time applications that require quick memory operations. Next, we discussed cache-aware programming, we improved spatial locality and increased the amount of useful data fetched into the cache. This restructuring improved data alignment with cache line boundaries, resulting in significant memory access time reductions and overall performance improvements.

Lastly, we gained skill of placement **new** and aligned memory allocations for managing the location of objects in memory during construction. These techniques were especially useful for optimizing memory access in systems with strict alignment requirements, such as those found in high-performance simulations or hardware-specific environments. The combination of these state-of-the-art memory management techniques improved cache utilization, gave users more say over memory allocation, and boosted performance for programs that need fast, low-latency memory operations.

CHAPTER 7: ADVANCED MULTITHREADING FOR EXPERTS

Overview

Here, in this chapter, we will look at the advanced aspects of multithreading in C++, where efficiently managing multiple threads can result in significant performance improvements. We will start by learning how to easily spawn and manage threads, giving you complete control over creating, managing, and terminating threads in a structured and efficient way. Then we will look at how to maximize parallelism by using mutexes and locks to prevent race conditions and ensure that threads access shared resources safely without causing data corruption or unpredictable behavior.

The next section focuses on using condition variables to control thread communication. Finally, we will look at how thread pools can help balance workload distribution and make better use of system resources by managing a pool of reusable threads that can handle multiple tasks at once. By mastering these concepts, you will be prepared to take on multithreading problems with authority.

Spawn and Command Threads Effortlessly

Multithreading allows programs to perform multiple tasks simultaneously by dividing work across multiple threads. Each thread operates independently, sharing the same process resources like memory but executing concurrently with other threads. This can significantly improve performance in applications that can parallelize tasks, such as data processing, simulations, and real-time systems. Here, we will explore to create, manage, and synchronize threads using the Standard Library's **std::thread** for efficient multithreaded programming.

Basic Thread Creation and Management

The **std::thread** class is the key component for creating and managing threads. Given below is a sample program of how to spawn a basic thread that performs a task in parallel with the main thread:

```
#include <iostream>

#include <thread>



void task() {

    std::cout << "Thread ID: " <<
std::this_thread::get_id() << " is running the task.\n";
```

```
}

int main() {
    // Spawn a new thread to run the task
    std::thread t1(task);

    // Print from the main thread
    std::cout << "Main thread ID: " <<
std::this_thread::get_id() << " is executing.\n";

    // Wait for the thread to finish
    t1.join();

    return 0;
}
```

In this, the function **task()** is a simple task that prints the thread ID. We use **std::thread** to create a new thread, **t1**, which runs this task concurrently with the main thread. The **join()** function is used to ensure that the main thread waits for **t1** to finish before continuing. Without **join()**, the main thread could terminate while **t1** is still running, potentially leaving unfinished tasks. The **std::this_thread::get_id()** returns the ID of the currently executing thread to distinguish between the main thread and the spawned thread.

Advanced Thread Management and Synchronization

When dealing with multiple threads, especially in performance-critical applications, you need to manage thread interactions carefully. Now, to demonstrate advanced thread management, we will improvise the previous example by spawning multiple threads, each performing a part of a larger task.

Sample Program: Spawning Multiple Threads

Let us say we want to perform a computation in parallel, dividing the work among several threads. So, for this, we will sum the elements of an array using multiple threads, each responsible for summing a portion of the array.

```
#include <iostream>

#include <thread>

#include <vector>

#include <numeric>  // For std::accumulate


// Function for each thread to sum a portion of the array

void partial_sum(const std::vector<int>& data, size_t start, size_t end, int& result) {

    result = std::accumulate(data.begin() + start, data.begin() + end, 0);

}


int main() {

    const size_t num_elements = 1000;

    const size_t num_threads = 4;


    // Generate an array of numbers

    std::vector<int> data(num_elements);
```

```
    for (size_t i = 0; i < num_elements; ++i) {
        data[i] = i + 1;  // Fill with numbers 1 to 1000
    }

    // Create threads and partial sum results
    std::vector<std::thread> threads;
    std::vector<int> results(num_threads, 0);  // Each
thread stores its partial result here
    size_t block_size = num_elements / num_threads;

    // Spawn threads to calculate partial sums
    for (size_t i = 0; i < num_threads; ++i) {
        size_t start = i * block_size;
        size_t end = (i == num_threads - 1) ?
num_elements : (i + 1) * block_size;
        threads.emplace_back(partial_sum, std::ref(data),
start, end, std::ref(results[i]));
    }

    // Wait for all threads to complete
    for (auto& t : threads) {
        t.join();
```

```
    }

    // Sum the partial results

    int total_sum = std::accumulate(results.begin(),
results.end(), 0);

    std::cout << "Total sum: " << total_sum << "\n";

    return 0;
}
```

Here, we divide the array **data** into **num_threads** parts, and this division of labor helps distribute the workload evenly across multiple CPU cores, improving performance for large datasets.

Also, we use **std::ref** to pass references to the vector **data** and the result **results[i]**. This ensures that each thread can modify its respective result without creating unnecessary copies of the data. Once all threads are spawned, the main thread waits for each one to complete using **join()**. This ensures that the final summation of partial results only happens after all threads have finished their work. After all threads complete, we use **std::accumulate()** to sum the results from each thread, obtaining the total sum of the array.

This entire thing demonstrates how spawning and synchronizing threads can improve performance for tasks that can be divided into smaller, independent units of work.

Thread Safety and Data Races

When multiple threads access shared resources (e.g., shared data or memory), we must ensure that their access is coordinated to prevent **data races**, where two or more threads access shared data simultaneously, leading to unpredictable behavior. For instance, if two threads try to write to the same memory location simultaneously, the final value of the data may depend on the order of execution, which is often non-deterministic in multithreaded programs.

In the above example, each thread works on separate parts of the array and has its own result storage (**results[i]**), so there is no shared memory conflict. However, in scenarios where threads must update shared data, mechanisms like mutexes and locks are required to ensure thread safety.

Spawning Threads for High-Performance Apps

In high-performance parallel applications, following techniques can be applied to further improve thread management in complex programs:

Thread Pooling

Rather than constantly creating and destroying threads, which can be expensive, thread pools allow you to maintain a fixed number of threads that can be reused for multiple tasks. This reduces the overhead of thread creation and destruction, especially in applications where tasks are small and frequent.

Task-based Parallelism

Instead of directly managing threads, modern C++ provides higher-level abstractions like **`std::async`** and **`std::future`** to handle asynchronous tasks. These abstractions allow the runtime to manage thread execution efficiently without requiring explicit thread management.

Load Balancing

If one thread finishes much earlier than others, some CPU cores may remain idle, reducing the overall efficiency of the program. Techniques like dynamic scheduling or adaptive partitioning can help balance the workload dynamically.

Sample Program: Dynamic Thread Spawning with 'std::async'

We can also use **`std::async`** to handle tasks asynchronously without manually creating and managing threads. The following example demonstrates the same parallel summation task using **`std::async`**:

```
#include <iostream>

#include <vector>

#include <numeric>

#include <future>  // For std::async and std::future


// Function for each thread to sum a portion of the array
```

```
int partial_sum(const std::vector<int>& data, size_t
start, size_t end) {
    return std::accumulate(data.begin() + start,
data.begin() + end, 0);
}

int main() {
    const size_t num_elements = 1000;
    const size_t num_threads = 4;

    // Generate an array of numbers
    std::vector<int> data(num_elements);
    for (size_t i = 0; i < num_elements; ++i) {
        data[i] = i + 1;  // Fill with numbers 1 to 1000
    }

    // Create futures to handle the partial sums
    std::vector<std::future<int>> futures;
    size_t block_size = num_elements / num_threads;

    // Spawn tasks asynchronously to calculate partial
sums
```

```
    for (size_t i = 0; i < num_threads; ++i) {
        size_t start = i * block_size;
        size_t end = (i == num_threads - 1) ?
num_elements : (i + 1) * block_size;
        futures.push_back(std::async(std::launch::async,
partial_sum, std::cref(data), start, end));
    }

    // Sum the results from each future
    int total_sum = 0;
    for (auto& future : futures) {
        total_sum += future.get();  // Wait for each task
to complete
    }

    std::cout << "Total sum: " << total_sum << "\n";

    return 0;
}
```

In this section, we demonstrated how to create, manage, and synchronize threads to achieve parallel execution, significantly improving performance in data-parallel tasks. Additionally, we explored advanced thread management techniques, such as task-based parallelism using **std::async** and dynamic thread spawning, which allow for more flexible and efficient multithreaded programming.

Unlock Parallelism with Mutexes and Locks

In multithreaded programming, one of the critical challenges is ensuring that multiple threads can access shared resources safely. When multiple threads attempt to modify or read shared data concurrently, it can lead to **race conditions** or **data corruption**, which can cause unpredictable and incorrect behavior. While mutexes and locks are powerful tools to ensure thread safety, improper use can lead to problems like **deadlock**, where two or more threads are stuck waiting for each other to release resources, causing the program to hang indefinitely. In this section, we will explore how to use mutexes and locks effectively, and demonstrate practical techniques to avoid common pitfalls, such as deadlocks and race conditions.

What are Mutexes and Locks?

A **mutex** is a synchronization primitive that prevents multiple threads from accessing shared resources simultaneously. When a thread locks a mutex, it gains exclusive access to the shared resource, and no other thread can acquire the same lock until the mutex is released.

A **lock** is a more general concept that represents the ownership of a mutex. C++ offers several types of locks, such as:

- **`std::lock_guard`**: Automatically acquires a mutex when it is created and releases it when it goes out of scope.
- **`std::unique_lock`**: More flexible than **`lock_guard`**, allowing manual locking and unlocking of the mutex.

These synchronization mechanisms can ensure that only one thread accesses shared data at a time, preventing race conditions.

Sample Program: Protecting Shared Data with a Mutex

We will start with a simple example to demonstrate the use of a mutex. Suppose we have two threads that increment a shared counter. Without proper synchronization, both threads may try to modify the counter at the same time, leading to incorrect results.

```
#include <iostream>

#include <thread>

#include <mutex>



int counter = 0;  // Shared resource
```

```
std::mutex mtx;   // Mutex to protect the shared resource

void increment() {
    for (int i = 0; i < 1000000; ++i) {
        std::lock_guard<std::mutex> lock(mtx);  // Lock
the mutex to prevent race conditions
        ++counter;
    }
}

int main() {
    std::thread t1(increment);
    std::thread t2(increment);

    t1.join();
    t2.join();

    std::cout << "Final counter value: " << counter <<
"\n";
    return 0;
}
```

Here,

- The **counter** variable is shared between both threads, and **mtx** is a mutex that will control access to the counter.
- Inside the **increment()** function, we use **std::lock_guard** to acquire the mutex before modifying the counter. This ensures that only one thread can increment the counter at a time. The lock is automatically released when the **lock_guard** goes out of scope, which happens at the end of each loop iteration.
- The **join()** calls ensure that both threads finish their execution before the program exits.In the above sample script, using a mutex prevents race conditions, ensuring that the final value of the counter is correct.

Sample Program: Avoiding Deadlock with Multiple Mutexes

In more complex programs, threads may need to acquire multiple locks to access different shared resources. If two threads try to lock resources in different orders, it can lead to a **deadlock**, where both threads are waiting for the other to release a resource, and neither can proceed.

Now for this, we will consider an example where two shared resources are protected by two mutexes. Check the following sample program demonstrating a potential deadlock situation:

```
#include <iostream>

#include <thread>

#include <mutex>


std::mutex mtx1;

std::mutex mtx2;


void task1() {

    std::lock_guard<std::mutex> lock1(mtx1);  // Lock
mtx1 first
```

```
std::this_thread::sleep_for(std::chrono::milliseconds(100
)); // Simulate some work

    std::lock_guard<std::mutex> lock2(mtx2); // Lock
mtx2 next

    std::cout << "Task 1 acquired both locks.\n";

}


void task2() {

    std::lock_guard<std::mutex> lock2(mtx2); // Lock
mtx2 first


std::this_thread::sleep_for(std::chrono::milliseconds(100
)); // Simulate some work

    std::lock_guard<std::mutex> lock1(mtx1); // Lock
mtx1 next

    std::cout << "Task 2 acquired both locks.\n";

}


int main() {

    std::thread t1(task1);

    std::thread t2(task2);


    t1.join();
```

```
    t2.join();


    return 0;
}
```

In the above program,

We lock **mtx1** first and then **mtx2** in **task1()**. And in **task2()**, we do the opposite: we lock **mtx2** first and then **mtx1**. If **task1()** locks **mtx1** and **task2()** locks **mtx2** at the same time, both threads will be waiting for the other to release the second lock, resulting in a deadlock.

The call to **std::this_thread::sleep_for()** simulates a delay between acquiring the first and second locks, making the deadlock scenario more likely. Now, to prevent deadlock, we must ensure that all threads acquire locks in the same order.

Avoiding Deadlock with 'std::lock()'

C++ provides **std::lock()** to safely lock multiple mutexes in a deadlock-free manner. It attempts to lock all the given mutexes simultaneously, ensuring that no thread will get stuck waiting for a resource held by another thread.

Given below is how we can modify the previous example to avoid deadlock using **std::lock()**:

```
#include <iostream>

#include <thread>

#include <mutex>


std::mutex mtx1;

std::mutex mtx2;


void task1() {
```

```
    // Lock both mutexes in a deadlock-free manner
    std::lock(mtx1, mtx2);

    // Use std::lock_guard to manage both locks
    std::lock_guard<std::mutex> lock1(mtx1,
std::adopt_lock);
    std::lock_guard<std::mutex> lock2(mtx2,
std::adopt_lock);

    std::cout << "Task 1 acquired both locks.\n";
}

void task2() {
    // Lock both mutexes in a deadlock-free manner
    std::lock(mtx1, mtx2);

    // Use std::lock_guard to manage both locks
    std::lock_guard<std::mutex> lock1(mtx1,
std::adopt_lock);
    std::lock_guard<std::mutex> lock2(mtx2,
std::adopt_lock);

    std::cout << "Task 2 acquired both locks.\n";
```

```
}


int main() {
    std::thread t1(task1);
    std::thread t2(task2);


    t1.join();
    t2.join();


    return 0;
}
```

Here, the call to **std::lock(mtx1, mtx2)** locks both **mtx1** and **mtx2** simultaneously. It handles the ordering of locks internally, so no thread can be left waiting indefinitely. After locking both mutexes with **std::lock()**, we use **std::lock_guard** with the **std::adopt_lock** tag. This tells **lock_guard** that the mutexes are already locked, so it does not need to lock them again. This ensures that the mutexes will be automatically released when the **lock_guard** objects go out of scope.

Sample Program: Avoid Race Condition using 'std::unique_lock'

Another common issue in multithreaded programs is the race condition, where two or more threads attempt to modify shared data concurrently. We can avoid race conditions using **std::unique_lock**, which offers more flexibility than **std::lock_guard** because it allows manual locking and unlocking of the mutex.

For this, we will modify the earlier counter example to use **std::unique_lock** instead of **std::lock_guard**:

```
#include <iostream>
```

```
#include <thread>
#include <mutex>


int counter = 0;
std::mutex mtx;


void increment() {
    for (int i = 0; i < 1000000; ++i) {
        std::unique_lock<std::mutex> lock(mtx);  // Lock
the mutex
        ++counter;
        // The lock can be explicitly unlocked or will
unlock when going out of scope
    }
}


int main() {
    std::thread t1(increment);
    std::thread t2(increment);


    t1.join();
    t2.join();
```

```
    std::cout << "Final counter value: " << counter <<
"\n";

    return 0;

}
```

In the above sample script, **std::unique_lock** offers more control over locking and unlocking the mutex, making it useful for situations where you need to lock and unlock the mutex multiple times within the same scope. However, improper use of mutexes can lead to deadlocks, where two or more threads wait indefinitely for each other to release resources.

Tame Thread Communication with Condition Variables

When working with multiple threads, there are often situations where threads need to communicate with each other or wait for certain conditions to be met before proceeding. One of the most efficient ways to manage this is through **condition variables.** A **condition variable** allows a thread to sleep and wait for a specific condition to become true. Another thread can signal the waiting thread when the condition is met, allowing it to resume execution. This mechanism is essential for scenarios such as producer-consumer models, where one thread produces data and another consumes it.

In this section, we will explore how condition variables work, demonstrate how to use them effectively, and build a practical multithreaded example that leverages condition variables to design efficient waiting mechanisms and signaling between threads.

How Condition Variables Work?

Condition variables work in conjunction with a **mutex** to control access to shared resources. Given below is the general process:

- A thread locks a mutex and checks whether a specific condition is true.
- If the condition is false, the thread calls **wait()** on the condition variable, which releases the mutex and puts the thread to sleep.
- Another thread modifies the shared data and calls **notify_one()** or **notify_all()** on the condition variable to signal waiting threads.

- The waiting thread wakes up, reacquires the mutex, and checks if the condition is now true. If it is, the thread proceeds; if not, it waits again.

The key advantage of condition variables is that they allow threads to sleep while waiting for a condition to change, rather than actively polling and consuming CPU resources.

Sample Program: Using Condition Variable

To understand it practically, we will create a simple producer-consumer scenario, where the producer thread generates data, and the consumer thread waits for the data to be produced before consuming it.

```
#include <iostream>

#include <thread>

#include <mutex>

#include <condition_variable>

#include <queue>


std::queue<int> data_queue;

std::mutex mtx;

std::condition_variable cv;

bool done = false;


void producer() {

    for (int i = 0; i < 10; ++i) {

        std::unique_lock<std::mutex> lock(mtx);

        data_queue.push(i);  // Produce data

        std::cout << "Produced: " << i << "\n";
```

```
        lock.unlock();
        cv.notify_one();  // Notify the consumer

std::this_thread::sleep_for(std::chrono::milliseconds(100
));  // Simulate work
    }
    // Signal that production is done
    std::unique_lock<std::mutex> lock(mtx);
    done = true;
    lock.unlock();
    cv.notify_one();  // Notify the consumer that
production is finished
}


void consumer() {
    while (true) {
        std::unique_lock<std::mutex> lock(mtx);
        cv.wait(lock, [] { return !data_queue.empty() ||
done; });  // Wait for data or done signal


        while (!data_queue.empty()) {
            int data = data_queue.front();
            data_queue.pop();
```

```
            std::cout << "Consumed: " << data << "\n";
        }

        if (done) break;
    }
}

int main() {
    std::thread prod(producer);
    std::thread cons(consumer);

    prod.join();
    cons.join();

    return 0;
}
```

In this, we use a **std::queue<int>** as the shared data structure for produced data. The **std::condition_variable cv** is used to synchronize the producer and consumer. The producer notifies the consumer when new data is available by calling **cv.notify_one()**, and the consumer waits on the condition variable using **cv.wait()**.

The **producer()** function generates numbers and pushes them to the queue. After adding data, it unlocks the mutex and notifies the consumer using **cv.notify_one()**. After producing 10 items, it sets the **done** flag to true and notifies the consumer one last time to signal that production is finished.

The **consumer()** function waits for data using **cv.wait()**. The **wait()** function releases the mutex and puts the thread to sleep until the condition variable is notified. Once data is available, the consumer processes it. When the **done** flag is set to true, the consumer stops waiting and finishes.

With this, it has illustrated how condition variables help threads wait for specific conditions without busy-waiting or consuming CPU resources. These condition variables become even more powerful in complex systems where multiple threads need to coordinate their actions. We will extend the producer-consumer example to a more advanced scenario where multiple producers and consumers work in parallel, but we want to ensure that the consumers do not consume data before it is fully produced.

In this case, we can use condition variables to efficiently manage the flow of communication between threads and prevent race conditions.

Sample Program: Multiple Producers and Consumers with Condition Variables

In the above program, we will have two producer threads generating data and two consumer threads consuming data. The condition variable ensures that consumers wait until data is available, and producers notify the consumers when data is ready.

```
#include <iostream>

#include <thread>

#include <mutex>

#include <condition_variable>

#include <queue>

#include <vector>


std::queue<int> data_queue;

std::mutex mtx;

std::condition_variable cv;
```

```
bool done = false;

int production_count = 0;  // Track the number of
produced items


// Producer function: Generates data and pushes it to the
queue

void producer(int producer_id, int num_items) {

    for (int i = 0; i < num_items; ++i) {

        std::unique_lock<std::mutex> lock(mtx);

        data_queue.push(i + (producer_id * 100));  //
Distinguish producer data

        std::cout << "Producer " << producer_id << "
produced: " << i + (producer_id * 100) << "\n";

        ++production_count;

        lock.unlock();

        cv.notify_one();  // Notify a consumer


std::this_thread::sleep_for(std::chrono::milliseconds(100
));  // Simulate work

    }



    // Signal that this producer is done producing

    std::unique_lock<std::mutex> lock(mtx);
```

```
    done = true;

    cv.notify_all();  // Notify all consumers that
production is finished

}


// Consumer function: Consumes data from the queue

void consumer(int consumer_id) {

    while (true) {

        std::unique_lock<std::mutex> lock(mtx);

        cv.wait(lock, [] { return !data_queue.empty() ||
done; });  // Wait for data or done signal

        while (!data_queue.empty()) {

            int data = data_queue.front();

            data_queue.pop();

            std::cout << "Consumer " << consumer_id << "
consumed: " << data << "\n";

        }


        if (done && data_queue.empty()) break;  // Exit
if done and no more data

    }

}
```

```
int main() {
    const int num_producers = 2;
    const int num_consumers = 2;
    const int items_per_producer = 5;

    // Create producer threads
    std::vector<std::thread> producers;
    for (int i = 0; i < num_producers; ++i) {
        producers.emplace_back(producer, i,
items_per_producer);
    }

    // Create consumer threads
    std::vector<std::thread> consumers;
    for (int i = 0; i < num_consumers; ++i) {
        consumers.emplace_back(consumer, i);
    }

    // Wait for producers to finish
    for (auto& prod : producers) {
        prod.join();
    }
```

```
    // Wait for consumers to finish
    for (auto& cons : consumers) {
        cons.join();
    }

    std::cout << "All producers and consumers have
finished.\n";
    return 0;
}
```

In this example,

- There are two producers, each generating five items. The **producer()** function pushes data to the queue and notifies the consumers using the condition variable. Each producer generates data that is distinct from the other to simulate different sources of data.
- There are two consumers that wait for data to become available using **cv.wait()**. Each consumer checks the condition variable and consumes the data when it is notified.
- The consumers wait efficiently using the condition variable, which ensures that they do not consume CPU resources while waiting for data to be produced. They only wake up when data is available or when all producers have finished.
- With the use of mutex and condition variable together, we ensure that access to the shared **data_queue** is thread-safe. The **cv.wait()** function automatically releases the mutex while the thread is waiting and reacquires it when the thread is notified.
- The **producer()** function calls **cv.notify_one()** after adding data to the queue, which wakes up one of the waiting consumer threads. Once all data has been produced, the producers signal completion using **cv.notify_all()**, which wakes up all remaining consumers to finish their work.

The elimination of busy-waiting and reduction in CPU use is achieved by enabling threads to sleep while waiting for a condition to change. Here, we showed how to avoid race problems and efficiently manage shared resources in a producer-consumer scenario by synchronizing several threads using condition variables.

Balance Load with Thread Pools

Background

In multithreaded applications, managing the creation and destruction of threads can introduce significant overhead, especially when tasks are small or frequent. Every time a new thread is created, resources are allocated, and once the thread finishes its task, those resources are deallocated. In performance-critical applications, this overhead can negate the benefits of multithreading. To address this issue, **thread pools** provide an efficient way to reuse a fixed number of threads, reducing the cost associated with constantly creating and destroying threads.

A **thread pool** maintains a set of threads that are ready to execute tasks. Instead of creating a new thread for each task, tasks are submitted to a queue, and the available threads in the pool pick them up for execution. This model allows better control over resource utilization, ensures that CPU cores are fully utilized, and helps balance the workload across multiple threads, leading to optimized performance.

Working of Thread Pool

A thread pool typically consists of the following components:

1. **A pool of threads**: A fixed number of threads are created when the thread pool is initialized. These threads wait for tasks to be assigned to them.
2. **A task queue**: Tasks (units of work) are submitted to the pool and placed in a queue. When a thread becomes available, it picks up a task from the queue and executes it.
3. **Task synchronization**: A condition variable or other synchronization mechanism is used to notify threads when new tasks are available in the queue.
4. **Load balancing**: The thread pool ensures that tasks are evenly distributed across threads, minimizing idle time and maximizing CPU utilization.

Sample Program: Designing a Thread Pool

We will design a thread pool for our multithreaded application. The thread pool will consist of worker threads that continuously fetch and execute tasks from a shared task queue. Once all tasks are processed, the thread pool will shut down gracefully.

Given below is the code for a simple thread pool:

```
#include <iostream>
```

```cpp
#include <vector>
#include <thread>
#include <queue>
#include <mutex>
#include <condition_variable>
#include <functional>
#include <atomic>

class ThreadPool {
public:
    ThreadPool(size_t num_threads);
    ~ThreadPool();

    // Add a new task to the thread pool
    void enqueue_task(std::function<void()> task);

    // Shutdown the thread pool
    void shutdown();

private:
```

```
    std::vector<std::thread> workers;                      //
Pool of worker threads

    std::queue<std::function<void()>> task_queue;  //
Queue of tasks

    std::mutex queue_mutex;                                //
Mutex to protect access to the task queue

    std::condition_variable cv;                            //
Condition variable to notify workers of new tasks

    std::atomic<bool> stop;                                //
Flag to indicate shutdown


    // Worker thread function

    void worker_thread();

};


// ThreadPool constructor: initializes worker threads

ThreadPool::ThreadPool(size_t num_threads) : stop(false)
{

    for (size_t i = 0; i < num_threads; ++i) {

        workers.emplace_back(&ThreadPool::worker_thread,
this);

    }

}
```

```
// ThreadPool destructor: shuts down the pool and joins
all threads

ThreadPool::~ThreadPool() {

    shutdown();

}


// Add a task to the task queue

void ThreadPool::enqueue_task(std::function<void()> task)
{

    {

        std::unique_lock<std::mutex> lock(queue_mutex);

        task_queue.push(std::move(task));  // Add the
task to the queue

    }

    cv.notify_one();  // Notify one worker thread

}


// Worker thread function: continuously fetch and execute
tasks

void ThreadPool::worker_thread() {

    while (true) {

        std::function<void()> task;
```

```
        // Fetch the next task from the queue
        {
            std::unique_lock<std::mutex>
lock(queue_mutex);
            cv.wait(lock, [this] { return stop ||
!task_queue.empty(); });

            if (stop && task_queue.empty()) return;  //
Exit if pool is stopped and no tasks are left

            task = std::move(task_queue.front());
            task_queue.pop();
        }

        // Execute the task
        task();
    }
}

// Shutdown the thread pool
void ThreadPool::shutdown() {
    {
```

```
        std::unique_lock<std::mutex> lock(queue_mutex);
        stop = true;  // Set the stop flag to true
    }

    cv.notify_all();  // Notify all worker threads to
finish
    for (std::thread &worker : workers) {
        if (worker.joinable()) {
            worker.join();  // Join each worker thread
        }
    }
}
```

In the above program,

- The **ThreadPool** constructor initializes the pool with the specified number of threads. Each worker thread runs the **worker_thread()** function, which continuously fetches tasks from the task queue.
- The **enqueue_task()** function allows external code to submit tasks to the pool. The task is then pushed onto the queue, and one of the worker threads is notified to wake up and process the task.
- Each worker thread continuously fetches tasks from the queue and executes them. If no tasks are available and the pool has not been stopped, the thread waits until a task is available. Once the **stop** flag is set to **true**, the worker threads stop fetching tasks and exit gracefully.
- The **shutdown()** function sets the **stop** flag to **true** and notifies all worker threads to finish their tasks. Once all threads complete their current tasks, the thread pool is shut down.

Sample Program: Implementing a Task for Thread Pool

Now, let us extend our producer-consumer scenario to use the thread pool. Here, we will have multiple tasks that simulate producers and consumers, and the thread pool will balance the load across multiple threads.

```
#include <iostream>

#include <thread>

#include <mutex>

#include <queue>

#include <chrono>

#include <condition_variable>

#include <functional>


// Global data structures

std::queue<int> data_queue;

std::mutex mtx;

std::condition_variable cv;

bool done = false;


// Task for producer: Generates data

void producer_task(int producer_id) {

    for (int i = 0; i < 5; ++i) {
```

```
std::this_thread::sleep_for(std::chrono::milliseconds(100
));  // Simulate work
        {
            std::unique_lock<std::mutex> lock(mtx);
            data_queue.push(i + producer_id * 100);  //
Produce data
            std::cout << "Producer " << producer_id << "
produced: " << i + producer_id * 100 << "\n";
        }
        cv.notify_one();  // Notify one consumer
    }

    {
        std::unique_lock<std::mutex> lock(mtx);
        done = true;  // Signal that production is done
    }
    cv.notify_all();
}

// Task for consumer: Consumes data
void consumer_task(int consumer_id) {
    while (true) {
```

```
        std::unique_lock<std::mutex> lock(mtx);
        cv.wait(lock, [] { return !data_queue.empty() ||
done; });

        while (!data_queue.empty()) {
            int data = data_queue.front();
            data_queue.pop();
            std::cout << "Consumer " << consumer_id << "
consumed: " << data << "\n";
        }

        if (done) break;
    }
}

int main() {
    // Create a thread pool with 4 threads
    ThreadPool pool(4);

    // Enqueue producer tasks
    pool.enqueue_task(std::bind(producer_task, 1));
    pool.enqueue_task(std::bind(producer_task, 2));
```

```
    // Enqueue consumer tasks
    pool.enqueue_task(std::bind(consumer_task, 1));
    pool.enqueue_task(std::bind(consumer_task, 2));

    // Allow the tasks to complete
    std::this_thread::sleep_for(std::chrono::seconds(3));

    // Shutdown the thread pool
    pool.shutdown();

    std::cout << "All tasks completed.\n";
    return 0;
}
```

In the above script, we create a **ThreadPool** with four worker threads. We then enqueue tasks to the pool using **pool.enqueue_task()**. The producer tasks generate data and push it to the queue, while the consumer tasks wait for data and process it. The worker threads in the pool pick up tasks from the queue and execute them concurrently. The thread pool ensures that tasks are distributed across available threads, balancing the load and making sure that no thread remains idle for long.

As in the previous examples, producers notify consumers when new data is available using a condition variable. Consumers wait for tasks to be produced and process them as soon as they become available. After all tasks have been enqueued, the **main()** thread waits for a few seconds to allow the tasks to complete, and then calls **pool.shutdown()** to stop the thread pool and join all worker threads. The **shutdown()** function sets the **stop** flag to **true**, notifies all worker threads, and waits for them to finish their current tasks before exiting. This ensures a graceful shutdown of the pool, where all tasks are processed before the program terminates.

Also, the thread pool distributes tasks across multiple worker threads, ensuring that the workload is balanced. Similarly, consumer tasks are executed in parallel, reducing idle time and maximizing CPU utilization. This balance allows the program to run more efficiently, particularly when there are multiple threads competing for system resources.

In real-world applications, thread pools can be further optimized by tuning the number of threads in the pool based on the system's capabilities. For example, a common approach is to set the number of threads to the number of CPU cores, ensuring that each core has one thread to execute, which prevents oversubscription and minimizes context switching overhead.

```
size_t num_threads = std::thread::hardware_concurrency();

ThreadPool pool(num_threads);
```

The **std::thread::hardware_concurrency()** function returns the number of hardware threads supported by the system, which helps determine an optimal number of threads for the pool. This way, you can dynamically adjust the size of the thread pool to match the system's capabilities and maximize performance.

This entire implementation demonstrated how thread pools can be used to balance the load in multithreaded applications, leading to better scalability, reduced overhead, and improved resource management. If you can master thread pools and load balancing, you can design robust multithreaded applications that fully utilize system resources while it maintains an optimal performance.

Summary

Briefly, this chapter began by teaching how to create and manage threads effortlessly using the **std::thread** class, demonstrating how to spawn and synchronize multiple threads to perform parallel tasks. The importance of using mutexes and locks was highlighted, which helped avoid race conditions when multiple threads accessed shared data. By using tools such as **std::lock_guard** and **std::unique_lock**, thread safety was ensured while minimizing performance bottlenecks.

The chapter further explained how to avoid deadlocks by controlling how threads acquire multiple locks, using **std::lock()** to safely manage the locking of multiple resources. Additionally, condition variables were introduced as a way to manage communication between threads. These allowed threads to wait efficiently for signals before resuming their tasks. It also included practical examples that demonstrated how to implement advanced waiting mechanisms and signal threads when certain conditions were met, such as in a producer-consumer model.

Finally, the concept of thread pools was explored as an effective way to balance workloads and reduce the overhead of frequent thread creation and destruction. A thread pool allowed multiple tasks to be queued and executed by a fixed number of threads, ensuring that system resources were used optimally while maintaining high performance. Through this approach, multithreaded applications could achieve better scalability and load balancing, making them more efficient in handling concurrent tasks.

CHAPTER 8: THREAD SYNCHRONIZATION AND ATOMIC MASTERY

Overview

This chapter explores advanced thread synchronization and atomic operation concepts, with a focus on methods that enable more efficient and dependable multithreading. We will start by simplifying thread synchronization techniques, with a focus on deadlock prevention and safe thread cooperation. Next, we will look at atomic operations, which enable threads to perform certain actions in an all-or-nothing fashion without the use of locks.

We will also look at how to orchestrate threads with futures, promises, and tasks, which provide higher-level abstractions for managing asynchronous tasks and communicating between threads. Finally, we will discuss lock-free data structures, which allow multiple threads to access and modify shared data without requiring locks, resulting in improved performance and scalability, especially in high-concurrency systems. Overall, you will learn advanced synchronization techniques in this chapter that will help you create multithreaded applications that are both efficient and feature-rich.

Thread Synchronization for Deadlocks

In today's multithreaded applications, deadlocks can arise in a variety of scenarios, from operating systems to large-scale distributed systems, database transactions, and real-time applications like game engines. These programs often rely on multiple threads or processes to handle tasks concurrently, making proper synchronization crucial. When threads wait indefinitely for resources to be freed, the entire program can become unresponsive, leading to crashes or severe performance degradation.

Underlying Causes of Deadlocks

There are four conditions, known as **Coffman's conditions**, that must be present for a deadlock to occur:

1. **Mutual Exclusion**: At least one resource is held in a non-shared mode, meaning only one thread can access the resource at a time. If another thread tries to access it, it must wait.
2. **Hold and Wait**: A thread is holding at least one resource while waiting to acquire additional resources that are currently held by other threads.
3. **No Preemption**: Resources cannot be forcibly taken away from a thread; they must be released voluntarily once the thread has completed its task.
4. **Circular Wait**: A circular chain of threads exists, where each thread holds one resource and waits for another resource held by the next thread in the chain.

These four conditions must all be true for a deadlock to occur. In most cases, the **circular wait** condition is the key factor, as it creates a cycle where no thread can proceed. Recognizing the presence of these conditions in a program is the first step in addressing the possibility of deadlocks.

Deadlocks Use-cases

Database Deadlocks

In database management systems, deadlocks often occur when multiple transactions attempt to lock different rows or tables at the same time. For example, if one transaction locks Row A and waits for Row B, while another transaction locks Row B and waits for Row A, a circular wait condition arises, and both transactions are deadlocked.

Operating Systems

In operating systems, deadlocks can happen when multiple processes require exclusive access to shared resources like memory, files, or devices. For example, two processes might each hold a different lock and wait for the other to release its lock, leading to a deadlock.

Multithreaded Applications

Deadlocks frequently occur in multithreaded programs where threads need to acquire multiple locks to perform certain operations. If threads acquire locks in different orders or hold locks while waiting for other locks, a deadlock can occur.

Deadlocks Avoidance Techniques

Deadlocks can be avoided by breaking one or more of Coffman's conditions. In this section, we will explore several advanced techniques that modern systems use to prevent deadlocks and design deadlock-free systems.

Resource Ordering

One of the most effective techniques for avoiding deadlocks is **resource ordering**. In this approach, all threads must acquire resources in a predefined global order. By ensuring that all threads lock resources in the same order, the circular wait condition is eliminated, as no thread will be waiting for a resource that is being held by another thread further down the chain.

For example, if threads need to lock resources A, B, and C, a global ordering rule could be established such that all threads must acquire locks in the order A -> B -> C. This ensures that no circular dependencies arise, as threads cannot request a lower-ordered resource after holding a higher-ordered one.

```
std::mutex mtxA, mtxB, mtxC;
```

```
// Thread 1 must lock in order A -> B -> C
void thread1() {
    std::lock_guard<std::mutex> lockA(mtxA);
    std::lock_guard<std::mutex> lockB(mtxB);
    std::lock_guard<std::mutex> lockC(mtxC);
    // Perform operations
}

// Thread 2 must also lock in order A -> B -> C
void thread2() {
    std::lock_guard<std::mutex> lockA(mtxA);
    std::lock_guard<std::mutex> lockB(mtxB);
    std::lock_guard<std::mutex> lockC(mtxC);
    // Perform operations
}
```

By enforcing a strict order in which locks are acquired, we prevent the circular wait condition and ensure that deadlocks do not occur.

Lock Hierarchies and Hierarchical Locking

Another approach is using **lock hierarchies**. This technique involves assigning a numeric or hierarchical value to each lock, and requiring that threads can only acquire locks in ascending order. Like resource ordering, lock hierarchies prevent circular waits by ensuring that threads cannot lock resources out of order.

Lock hierarchies are especially useful in systems with complex resource dependencies. For instance, in a system where certain locks are considered more critical than others, the more critical locks are assigned lower hierarchical values. Threads can acquire multiple locks as long as they only lock resources with higher hierarchical values after locking those with lower values.

Deadlock Detection with Timed Locks

Deadlock detection involves allowing deadlocks to occur but detecting them when they happen and resolving them by forcefully terminating one of the threads involved in the deadlock. While not ideal in all scenarios, deadlock detection is useful in systems like database management systems where transactions can be rolled back safely.

A subtler form of deadlock detection is timed locks. In C++, **std::timed_mutex** allows a thread to attempt to acquire a lock within a specified time period. If the thread cannot acquire the lock in the allotted time, it gives up and moves on, potentially trying again later. This prevents threads from blocking indefinitely and reduces the likelihood of deadlock.

```
#include <iostream>

#include <thread>

#include <mutex>

#include <chrono>


std::timed_mutex timed_mtx;


void task(int id) {

    if
(timed_mtx.try_lock_for(std::chrono::milliseconds(100)))
{

        std::cout << "Thread " << id << " acquired the
lock.\n";


std::this_thread::sleep_for(std::chrono::milliseconds(200
));

        timed_mtx.unlock();
```

```
    } else {
        std::cout << "Thread " << id << " could not
acquire the lock in time.\n";
    }
}

int main() {
    std::thread t1(task, 1);
    std::thread t2(task, 2);

    t1.join();
    t2.join();

    return 0;
}
```

In the above sample script, each thread attempts to acquire a timed lock. If the thread cannot acquire the lock within 100 milliseconds, it moves on without blocking indefinitely. This technique can prevent threads from waiting forever, thus reducing the chance of a deadlock occurring.

Thread Priority Inversion and Priority Inheritance

Deadlocks can also be caused by **thread priority inversion**, where a high-priority thread is blocked by a lower-priority thread holding a needed resource. In systems that rely heavily on thread prioritization, such as real-time systems, priority inversion can cause performance bottlenecks and lead to deadlocks.

To combat this, modern systems implement **priority inheritance**, where the priority of a low-priority thread holding a resource is temporarily increased to match the priority of the blocked high-priority thread. This ensures that the lower-priority thread finishes its task more quickly and releases the resource, allowing the high-priority thread to proceed.

```
// Simulating priority inversion scenario

// Priority inheritance would boost the priority of the
low-priority thread holding the lock.
```

While C++ does not directly provide support for priority inheritance, many operating systems and real-time scheduling libraries implement this technique to avoid deadlocks in priority-based scheduling systems.

Additionally, techniques like priority inheritance and lock-free data structures provide even more ways to manage thread synchronization efficiently, ensuring that multithreaded systems remain responsive, scalable, and high-performing.

Execute Atomic Operations with Precision

Atomic operations are operations that are performed as a single, indivisible step. In C++, atomic operations are provided by the **std::atomic** class template, which ensures that read-modify-write operations on variables are performed atomically. This means that no other thread can interrupt or interfere with the operation, ensuring thread safety without the need for traditional locking mechanisms.

Here, we will design highly efficient concurrent algorithms using atomic operations in our sample program, demonstrating how atomic operations help avoid the overhead of traditional locks while maintaining thread safety and improving performance.

Atomic Operations Overview

The key advantage of atomic operations is that they provide lock-free synchronization. This allows threads to modify shared data without the need to acquire and release locks, reducing contention between threads and improving overall system performance.

C++ provides a variety of atomic types and operations, including:

- **std::atomic<int>**: An atomic integer type that supports atomic increments, decrements, and other operations.
- **fetch_add()** and **fetch_sub()**: Atomically adds or subtracts a value from a variable.

- **`compare_exchange_weak()`** and **`compare_exchange_strong()`**: Atomically compares and exchanges values based on specific conditions.
- **Memory ordering**: Control over memory ordering using relaxed, acquire, and release semantics.

Now, we will apply these atomic operations to a practical scenario where we need to manage shared resources efficiently in a multithreaded program.

Sample Program: Using Atomic Operations in a Counter

We will take the example of a shared counter that multiple threads increment concurrently. Traditionally, we might use a mutex to protect access to the counter, ensuring that only one thread can modify the counter at a time. However, using a mutex introduces locking overhead, especially if many threads are competing for access. But by switching to atomic operations, we can eliminate the need for locks while ensuring that the counter is incremented safely by multiple threads.

Given below is how we can implement an atomic counter using **`std::atomic`**:

```
#include <iostream>

#include <thread>

#include <vector>

#include <atomic>


std::atomic<int> atomic_counter(0);  // Atomic counter
variable


void increment_counter(int num_iterations) {

    for (int i = 0; i < num_iterations; ++i) {

        atomic_counter.fetch_add(1);  // Atomically
increment the counter

    }
```

```
}

int main() {

    const int num_threads = 4;

    const int iterations_per_thread = 1000000;


    // Create threads to increment the atomic counter

    std::vector<std::thread> threads;

    for (int i = 0; i < num_threads; ++i) {

        threads.emplace_back(increment_counter,
iterations_per_thread);

    }


    // Join all threads

    for (auto& thread : threads) {

        thread.join();

    }


    std::cout << "Final counter value: " <<
atomic_counter.load() << "\n";


    return 0;

}
```

In the above program,

- The **std::atomic<int>** type ensures that the counter can be incremented atomically by multiple threads. This eliminates the need for locks, as the atomic operations guarantee that the counter is modified safely, even when accessed by multiple threads simultaneously.
- The **fetch_add()** function is used to atomically increment the counter by 1. This function ensures that no other thread can interfere with the operation, meaning the counter will always be updated correctly, regardless of how many threads are incrementing it.
- We create four threads, each of which increments the counter one million times. By using atomic operations, we avoid the overhead of locking and unlocking a mutex, which would otherwise slow down the program as threads wait for each other to release the lock.

After all threads finish their work, the final value of the counter is printed. The use of atomic operations ensures that the final counter value is correct, even though multiple threads were modifying the counter concurrently.

Advanced Atomic Operations using Compare-and-Swap

In addition to basic atomic operations like **fetch_add()**, atomic operations can also be used to implement more complex synchronization mechanisms. One of the most powerful atomic operations is compare-and-swap (CAS), which allows a thread to conditionally update a shared variable based on its current value. This operation is particularly useful in designing lock-free data structures and algorithms.

The **compare_exchange_weak()** and **compare_exchange_strong()** functions implement CAS. They compare the current value of an atomic variable to an expected value, and if they match, the variable is updated. Otherwise, the operation fails, and the thread can retry.

Following is a sample program of using CAS to implement a simple lock-free algorithm:

```
#include <iostream>

#include <thread>

#include <atomic>



std::atomic<int> shared_value(0);
```

```
void compare_and_swap_task() {
    int expected_value = 0;
    int new_value = 100;

    if
(shared_value.compare_exchange_strong(expected_value,
new_value)) {
        std::cout << "Thread successfully updated shared
value to " << shared_value.load() << "\n";
    } else {
        std::cout << "Thread failed to update shared
value. Current value: " << shared_value.load() << "\n";
    }
}

int main() {
    std::thread t1(compare_and_swap_task);
    std::thread t2(compare_and_swap_task);

    t1.join();
    t2.join();

    return 0;
```

```
}
```

Here, the **`compare_exchange_strong()`** function atomically compares the current value of **`shared_value`** to **`expected_value`**. If the values match, **`shared_value`** is updated to **`new_value`**. If another thread has already updated **`shared_value`**, the operation fails, and the thread can retry or take other action.

By using atomic operations, we demonstrated how an atomic counter allows multiple threads to increment a shared variable concurrently without the need for a mutex. We also explored more advanced atomic operations like compare-and-swap, which enable the design of lock-free algorithms and data structures.

Orchestrate Threads with Futures, Promises, and Tasks

Futures, Promises, and Tasks

Futures, **promises**, and **tasks** provide high-level abstractions that allow threads to communicate effectively, enabling clean synchronization of asynchronous operations. These constructs provide a flexible way to handle asynchronous computation, making it easier to coordinate and retrieve results from different threads. Futures and promises work together in a complementary manner. A **promise** is used to set a value that will be computed by a thread or some other task. This value is then accessed by the corresponding **future**, which waits for the result to become available. Once the computation is completed, the future retrieves the result, allowing different threads or tasks to be synchronized.

In asynchronous programming, a **future** represents a value that will be available at some point in the future. It provides a way to access the result of an asynchronous operation. A **promise**, on the other hand, is the counterpart that sets the value of the future once the asynchronous operation is complete. When a thread or function completes its task, it fulfills the promise, which makes the result available to the future.

The C++ Standard Library provides the following key constructs:

- **`std::future`**: Retrieves the result of an asynchronous operation once it is complete.
- **`std::promise`**: Allows a thread to set a result that will be retrieved by the future.
- **`std::async`**: Launches a task asynchronously and returns a future to access the result later.

- **std::packaged_task**: Wraps a function or callable object, allowing it to be run asynchronously and its result to be accessed through a future.

We will apply these concepts in our sample program by orchestrating threads to perform asynchronous tasks. We will demonstrate how futures and promises help synchronize different threads while ensuring that results are available when needed, without blocking or introducing unnecessary delays.

Sample Program: Asynchronous Computation with Futures and Promises

Consider a scenario where multiple threads perform parts of a computation, and the results of these computations need to be gathered and synchronized at the end. We can use futures and promises to achieve this cleanly as shown below:

```
#include <iostream>

#include <thread>

#include <future>

#include <vector>


// A function that performs a computation and returns the result via a promise

void compute_value(std::promise<int>&& promise, int value) {


std::this_thread::sleep_for(std::chrono::milliseconds(100));  // Simulate some work

    promise.set_value(value * value);  // Compute the square and set the result

}
```

```
int main() {
    const int num_threads = 4;
    std::vector<std::future<int>> futures;
    std::vector<std::promise<int>> promises(num_threads);

    // Spawn threads to perform computations
asynchronously
    for (int i = 0; i < num_threads; ++i) {
        // Move the promise into the thread and get the
corresponding future
        futures.push_back(promises[i].get_future());
        std::thread(compute_value,
std::move(promises[i]), i + 1).detach();
    }

    // Wait for all futures to be ready and print the
results
    for (auto& future : futures) {
        std::cout << "Computed value: " << future.get()
<< "\n";  // Wait for the result
    }

    return 0;
```

```
}
```

Here,

- Each thread is associated with a **std::promise** and a corresponding **std::future**. The promise is used to set the result of a computation, and the future is used to retrieve the result once the computation is complete. Here, we create four promises, and each promise is moved into a separate thread.
- The **compute_value()** function simulates some work (by sleeping for 100 milliseconds) and then sets the computed result in the promise. The result is the square of the input value.
- The main thread waits for all the futures to become ready using **future.get()**. This call blocks until the corresponding promise sets a value, ensuring that the result is available before proceeding. Once the result is ready, it is printed to the console.

This simple example illustrates how futures and promises can be used to synchronize multiple threads and retrieve the results of asynchronous computations without blocking unnecessarily.

Using std::async for High-Level Thread Orchestration

In addition to promises and futures, C++ provides the std::async function, which simplifies the process of launching asynchronous tasks. Unlike promises, **std::async** directly returns a future associated with the result of the asynchronous task.

We will modify the previous example to use **std::async** instead of manually managing promises and threads as shown below:

```
#include <iostream>

#include <future>

#include <vector>


// A function that performs a computation asynchronously

int compute_value(int value) {
```

```
std::this_thread::sleep_for(std::chrono::milliseconds(100
)); // Simulate some work

    return value * value; // Compute the square and
return the result

}


int main() {

    const int num_threads = 4;

    std::vector<std::future<int>> futures;


    // Launch tasks asynchronously using std::async

    for (int i = 0; i < num_threads; ++i) {

        futures.push_back(std::async(std::launch::async,
compute_value, i + 1));

    }


    // Wait for all futures to be ready and print the
results

    for (auto& future : futures) {

        std::cout << "Computed value: " << future.get()
<< "\n"; // Wait for the result

    }
```

```
    return 0;

}
```

In the above program, the **std::async** function launches the **compute_value()** function asynchronously and returns a future associated with the result. By passing **std::launch::async**, we explicitly request asynchronous execution (as opposed to deferred execution, which could happen if we used the default launch policy).

Combining Futures, Promises, and Tasks

In more complex scenarios, futures, promises, and tasks can be combined to build sophisticated workflows where multiple asynchronous tasks depend on each other. For example, the result of one asynchronous task might be used as input for another task, and so on. This can be achieved by chaining futures or coordinating multiple tasks with promises.

We will extend our sample program to demonstrate a scenario where the result of one task is used to trigger the execution of another task:

```
#include <iostream>

#include <thread>

#include <future>

#include <functional>


// A function that performs the first computation asynchronously

int compute_initial(int value) {


std::this_thread::sleep_for(std::chrono::milliseconds(100));  // Simulate some work

    return value * value;
```

```
}

// A function that depends on the result of the first
computation
int compute_final(int initial_result) {

std::this_thread::sleep_for(std::chrono::milliseconds(50)
); // Simulate additional work
    return initial_result + 10;
}

int main() {
    // Launch the first task using std::async
    std::future<int> initial_future =
std::async(std::launch::async, compute_initial, 5);

    // Wait for the first task to complete and use its
result for the second task
    int final_result =
compute_final(initial_future.get());

    // Output the final result
    std::cout << "Final computed value: " << final_result
<< "\n";
```

```
    return 0;
}
```

Here, the first task, **`compute_initial()`**, performs an initial computation asynchronously using **`std::async`**. The result of this task is retrieved using the future (**`initial_future.get()`**), which waits for the result to be ready.

The result of the first task is then passed to the **`compute_final()`** function, which performs additional work based on the result. This illustrates how asynchronous tasks can be chained together, with the result of one task feeding into the next.

Futures, promises, and tasks provide powerful tools for orchestrating asynchronous operations in multithreaded applications. By using these constructs, we demonstrated how futures and promises can be used to manage asynchronous computations, and how **`std::async`** simplifies the process of launching tasks asynchronously.

Build Lock-Free Data Structures for Ultimate Performance

What Makes Data Structures Lock-Free?

Lock-free data structures offer a powerful alternative to traditional thread synchronization mechanisms. **Lock-free data structures** eliminate the need for locks entirely by ensuring that multiple threads can concurrently modify shared data structures without causing data corruption, reducing contention and improving performance. These structures rely on atomic operations, which allow threads to perform updates in an all-or-nothing manner, without blocking each other.

A data structure is considered **lock-free** if multiple threads can operate on it concurrently without using locks, and at least one thread makes progress at any time. In other words, lock-free structures guarantee that system progress is not hindered by any individual thread. This makes them especially suitable for systems where high concurrency is expected, such as real-time systems, databases, and network applications.

Sample Program: Building a Lock-Free Stack

In this section, we will build a simple lock-free data structure and demonstrate how it eliminates the overhead associated with traditional locking mechanisms. Specifically, we will implement a lock-free stack using atomic operations, allowing multiple threads to push and pop elements concurrently.

We will start by building a simple lock-free stack using **std::atomic** and the compare-and-swap (CAS) operation. A stack is a common data structure that operates on a last in, first out (LIFO) basis, where elements are pushed onto the stack and popped off in reverse order. In a multithreaded environment, multiple threads may push and pop elements concurrently, leading to potential data races if not properly synchronized. Using CAS, we can ensure that push and pop operations are performed atomically, allowing multiple threads to modify the stack concurrently without locking.

Given below is a sample implementation of a lock-free stack in C++:

```
#include <iostream>

#include <atomic>

#include <thread>

#include <vector>



template <typename T>

class LockFreeStack {

private:

    struct Node {

        T data;

        Node* next;

        Node(T value) : data(value), next(nullptr) {}

    };



    std::atomic<Node*> head;  // Atomic pointer to the
head of the stack
```

```
public:
    LockFreeStack() : head(nullptr) {}

    // Push a new value onto the stack
    void push(T value) {
        Node* new_node = new Node(value);
        new_node->next = head.load();  // Set the new
node's next pointer to the current head

        // Atomically update the head to point to the new
node
        while (!head.compare_exchange_weak(new_node-
>next, new_node)) {
            // If the head changed, retry with the
updated head value
        }
    }

    // Pop a value from the stack
    bool pop(T& result) {
        Node* old_head = head.load();
```

```
        // Try to atomically update the head to the next
node

        while (old_head &&
!head.compare_exchange_weak(old_head, old_head->next)) {

            // Retry if the head was modified by another
thread

        }


        if (old_head) {

            result = old_head->data;  // Retrieve the
data from the old head

            delete old_head;          // Free the memory
for the old head

            return true;

        }


        return false;  // Stack was empty

    }


    // Check if the stack is empty

    bool empty() const {

        return head.load() == nullptr;

    }
```

```
};
```

In the above implementation,

- To push a value onto the stack, we first create a new node. The **next** pointer of the new node is set to point to the current head of the stack. Using **compare_exchange_weak()**, we then attempt to atomically update the **head** pointer to point to the new node. If another thread modifies the **head** during this time (i.e., another push or pop operation), the operation is retried with the updated value of **head**.
- To pop a value from the stack, we first load the current value of **head**. We then attempt to update **head** to point to the next node in the stack, using **compare_exchange_weak()**. If another thread modifies the **head** during this time, the operation is retried. If the stack is not empty, the value at the top is returned, and the node is deleted. If the stack is empty, the operation returns **false**.
- And then, by using atomic operations and CAS, we ensure that both push and pop operations are lock-free, meaning that threads can operate on the stack concurrently without blocking each other. The compare-and-swap operation ensures that no thread can leave the stack in an inconsistent state, even in the presence of concurrent updates.

Lock-free data structures provide significant performance benefits, including reduced contention, improved scalability, and lower latency, making them ideal for high-concurrency systems where performance is critical. By mastering lock-free programming techniques, one can build more efficient, scalable, and high-performance applications.

Summary

To sum up, this chapter took us to advanced thread synchronization techniques and atomic operations for designing efficient, high-performance multithreaded systems. It began with an exploration of deadlocks, explaining the underlying causes and offering solutions such as resource ordering, lock hierarchies, and timed locks to prevent threads from becoming stuck waiting on each other. The role of **std::lock()** was demonstrated to handle multiple locks safely, ensuring deadlock-free execution when working with shared resources.

Next, atomic operations were introduced as a method for achieving lock-free synchronization. By leveraging atomic variables and functions such as **compare_exchange_strong()** and **fetch_add()**, we demonstrated how concurrent algorithms could avoid the overhead of traditional locks. The chapter also delved into the use of futures, promises, and tasks for orchestrating asynchronous operations. The **std::async** construct was introduced as a high-level way to manage asynchronous tasks with minimal effort, enabling simple yet powerful thread coordination. Finally, the construction of lock-free data structures was explored with the implementation of a lock-free stack. This demonstrated how atomic operations allow multiple threads to push and pop data concurrently without using locks, eliminating locking overhead and improving performance in systems with high concurrency.

Chapter 9: Turbocharging Floats and Ints

Overview

In this chapter, we will explore advanced techniques for handling floating-point and integer operations, focusing on precision, performance, and control. We will begin by understanding **arbitrary precision arithmetic**, which allows us to perform calculations with precision beyond the limits of built-in types. This is essential for applications like cryptography or high-precision simulations. Then, we will look at ways to **optimize arithmetic operations**, enhancing performance by leveraging advanced CPU features and modern compiler optimizations.

Next, we will shift our focus to **fixed-point arithmetic**, a method that provides greater control over decimal precision while avoiding the pitfalls of floating-point inaccuracies. Finally, we will explore **mathematical constants and rounding,** learning how to work with constants like π and e, and how to precisely manage rounding strategies to meet the requirements of various mathematical applications. By mastering these techniques, we will be equipped to handle numeric computations with precision and efficiency.

Arbitrary Precision Arithmetic

Concept and Its Use

Arbitrary precision arithmetic refers to a computational technique that allows operations on numbers that exceed the precision limits of standard data types such as **`float`** and **`double`**. In traditional floating-point arithmetic, the precision is fixed by the number of bits allocated to represent the number, which can lead to rounding errors, overflow, or underflow when dealing with very large or very small numbers. Arbitrary precision eliminates these constraints, allowing numbers to be represented and manipulated with as much precision as necessary for the task at hand.

This approach is particularly useful in fields like scientific computing, cryptography, and high-precision financial calculations, where the limitations of built-in types like **`float`** and **`double`** are insufficient to maintain the accuracy required by the problem. Arbitrary precision is typically implemented via specialized libraries, such as the GNU Multiple Precision Arithmetic Library (GMP), which allows programmers to represent numbers with thousands or even millions of digits.

Benefits of Arbitrary Precision Arithmetic

Using arbitrary precision arithmetic in our planetary orbit simulation allows us to overcome the precision limitations of standard floating-point types, ensuring that the simulation remains accurate even over long time periods. This is crucial in scientific computing, where small errors can accumulate over time and lead to significantly incorrect results.

Key benefits include:

- **Avoidance of Rounding Errors**: With standard floating-point types, rounding errors can accumulate over time, especially in simulations that involve many iterations or very small changes in values. Arbitrary precision eliminates this issue by providing as much precision as necessary for the calculation.
- **Increased Accuracy**: By using arbitrary precision, we can simulate scenarios that require extremely high accuracy, such as the precise calculation of celestial bodies' orbits or quantum mechanical systems.
- **Flexible Precision**: One of the main advantages of arbitrary precision arithmetic is the ability to adjust the precision based on the problem's requirements. In some cases, we may need only a few extra bits of precision, while in others, we may need thousands of bits.

We will consider a scientific computing scenario where arbitrary precision arithmetic is crucial: calculating the orbits of planets over long time periods.

Sample Program: Planetary Orbit Simulation

Imagine we are working on a simulation to predict the orbits of planets over thousands or even millions of years. The gravitational interactions between planets and other celestial bodies are extremely sensitive to small changes in position and velocity. Using standard **`double`** precision for these calculations may lead to cumulative rounding errors, which over long periods can cause significant inaccuracies in the predicted orbits.

In this situation, arbitrary precision arithmetic is necessary to ensure that even the smallest differences in position or velocity are captured accurately, preventing errors from accumulating and distorting the results. We will demonstrate how we can use arbitrary precision arithmetic to handle this scenario.

For this example, we will use the **GMP** library, which provides support for arbitrary precision integers, rational numbers, and floating-point numbers. To use GMP, you will need to install it and link it with your C++ project. In our demonstration, we will focus on arbitrary precision floating-point numbers.

Following is how we can set up GMP in a C++ program to perform high-precision calculations:

```
#include <iostream>

#include <gmpxx.h>  // Include the GMP C++ interface



int main() {
```

```
    // Initialize arbitrary precision floating-point
numbers

    mpf_class planet_position(0.0, 256);  // 256 bits of
precision

    mpf_class planet_velocity(0.0, 256);  // 256 bits of
precision


    // Set initial conditions for the simulation

    planet_position = "1.496e11";  // Initial position of
1.496 x 10^11 meters (approx distance from Earth to Sun)

    planet_velocity = "30000";     // Initial velocity of
30,000 meters per second


    // Perform some calculations using arbitrary
precision arithmetic

    mpf_class time_step("1e5", 256);  // Time step of
100,000 seconds

    mpf_class gravitational_constant("6.67430e-11", 256);
// Gravitational constant in m^3 kg^-1 s^-2

    mpf_class mass_of_sun("1.989e30", 256);  // Mass of
the sun in kilograms


    // Calculate the gravitational force and update the
planet's position
```

```
    mpf_class force = (gravitational_constant *
mass_of_sun) / (planet_position * planet_position);

    planet_velocity += force * time_step;

    planet_position += planet_velocity * time_step;


    // Output the updated position and velocity with high
precision

    std::cout << "Updated position: " <<
planet_position.get_str(10) << " meters\n";

    std::cout << "Updated velocity: " <<
planet_velocity.get_str(10) << " meters/second\n";


    return 0;

}
```

Here, we declare two variables, **planet_position** and **planet_velocity**, using the **mpf_class** type provided by GMP. These variables are initialized with 256 bits of precision, far exceeding the precision of a **double**.

The initial position is set to approximately the distance from the Earth to the Sun (**1.496e11** meters), and the initial velocity is set to **30,000** meters per second. These are typical values for planetary orbit simulations.

The gravitational force is calculated using Newton's law of gravitation, where the force between two masses is inversely proportional to the square of the distance between them. The time step for the simulation is set to 100,000 seconds to simulate the movement of the planet over time.

The updated position and velocity are printed with high precision, using **get_str()** to output the values with full accuracy.

Sample Program: Arbitrary Precision in Financial Calculations

While the above example focuses on scientific computing, arbitrary precision arithmetic is also essential in financial applications where accuracy is critical. For example, in high-frequency trading systems or large-scale financial simulations, even small rounding errors can lead to significant financial losses. Following is an example where arbitrary precision arithmetic is used to calculate compound interest over a long period with very high precision:

```
#include <iostream>

#include <gmpxx.h>


int main() {

    // Initialize arbitrary precision floating-point
numbers for financial calculations

    mpf_class principal("10000.0", 256);  // Initial
principal of $10,000

    mpf_class rate("0.05", 256);          // Annual
interest rate of 5%

    mpf_class years("50", 256);           // Investment
period of 50 years


    // Calculate compound interest: A = P * (1 + r)^t

    mpf_class multiplier = 1.0 + rate;

    mpf_class final_amount = principal * pow(multiplier,
years.get_d());


    // Output the final amount after 50 years with high
precision
```

```
    std::cout << "Final amount after 50 years: $" <<
final_amount.get_str(10) << "\n";

    return 0;
}
```

Here, the **principal** is set to $10,000, with an annual interest rate of 5% and an investment period of 50 years. These values are stored as arbitrary precision floating-point numbers using the GMP library. The compound interest formula, **A=P*(1+r)^t**, is used to calculate the final amount after 50 years. Since the calculation involves raising a number to a power, the extra precision ensures that the result is accurate even for long investment periods.

The final amount is printed with high precision, ensuring that even the smallest fractional amounts are accurately represented. To conclude, the use of the GMP library eliminated the precision limitations of standard floating-point types, ensuring that our calculations remained accurate even in high-stakes simulations.

Warp Arithmetic Operations into High Gear

Standard implementations of mathematical operations may not always be optimized for the performance and speed required in these cases. By designing and utilizing **efficient algorithms**, we can handle complex mathematical operations at high speeds while maintaining accuracy. In this section, the focus will be on implementing algorithms that can handle these operations efficiently to warp these operations into high gear.

We will imagine we are working on a **real-time physics simulation** that computes the trajectory of objects in a 3D space. The simulation involves solving Newtonian motion equations, which require frequent trigonometric calculations (like sine, cosine, and tangent) as well as vector and matrix operations for transforming the position and orientation of objects. These operations must be performed quickly, as the simulation runs in real time, meaning that any delays in computation could lead to visible lag or incorrect simulation results.

To meet the real-time requirements, we need to ensure that the mathematical operations used in the simulation are optimized for speed without sacrificing accuracy.

Efficient Algorithms for Mathematical Operations

The key to optimizing mathematical operations lies in leveraging efficient algorithms that reduce unnecessary calculations and take advantage of modern CPU capabilities, such as parallel processing and vectorization. In this section, we will demonstrate how to implement efficient versions of some common mathematical operations, including matrix multiplication and trigonometric calculations.

Optimizing Matrix Multiplication

Matrix multiplication is a common operation in physics simulations, especially when dealing with transformations and rotations in 3D space. A naive implementation of matrix multiplication can be quite slow, particularly for large matrices. However, by optimizing the algorithm and making use of efficient computation techniques, we can significantly speed up the operation.

We will first implement a standard matrix multiplication algorithm, and then optimize it.

```
#include <iostream>

#include <vector>


// Function to perform matrix multiplication

void matrix_multiply(const
std::vector<std::vector<double>>& A, const
std::vector<std::vector<double>>& B,
std::vector<std::vector<double>>& C) {

    int n = A.size();

    for (int i = 0; i < n; ++i) {

        for (int j = 0; j < n; ++j) {

            C[i][j] = 0;

            for (int k = 0; k < n; ++k) {

                C[i][j] += A[i][k] * B[k][j];

            }

        }
```

```
    }
}
int main() {
    // Initialize two 3x3 matrices
    std::vector<std::vector<double>> A = {
        {1.0, 2.0, 3.0},
        {4.0, 5.0, 6.0},
        {7.0, 8.0, 9.0}
    };
    std::vector<std::vector<double>> B = {
        {9.0, 8.0, 7.0},
        {6.0, 5.0, 4.0},
        {3.0, 2.0, 1.0}
    };
    std::vector<std::vector<double>> C(3,
std::vector<double>(3));
    // Perform matrix multiplication
    matrix_multiply(A, B, C);
    // Output the result
    std::cout << "Resulting matrix:\n";
    for (const auto& row : C) {
        for (double val : row) {
```

```
            std::cout << val << " ";
        }
        std::cout << "\n";
    }

    return 0;
}
```

In the above example, we have implemented the naive matrix multiplication algorithm. The matrix multiplication operation is performed using three nested loops:

- The outer loop iterates over the rows of matrix **A**.
- The second loop iterates over the columns of matrix **B**.
- The innermost loop multiplies and sums the corresponding elements of matrices **A** and **B**.

This basic algorithm works, but it is not optimized for performance, especially when dealing with larger matrices. The algorithm's time complexity is **O(n3)O(n^3)O(n3)**, which can be prohibitively slow for large matrices.

Optimizing Matrix Multiplication Algorithm

To speed up the matrix multiplication, we can apply several optimization techniques, such as loop unrolling, blocking (also known as tiling), and leveraging SIMD (Single Instruction, Multiple Data) instructions available in modern processors.

- **Blocking (Tiling)**: Instead of processing one element at a time, we divide the matrices into smaller blocks and process them in chunks. This technique improves cache usage by ensuring that data is reused before it is evicted from the cache, thereby reducing memory access times.
- **SIMD Instructions**: Modern CPUs support SIMD instructions, which allow a single instruction to operate on multiple data points simultaneously. By leveraging SIMD, we can perform multiple arithmetic operations in parallel, significantly speeding up the matrix multiplication.

We will implement a more optimized version of the matrix multiplication algorithm using blocking:

```
#include <iostream>

#include <vector>

#include <cmath>



// Function to perform matrix multiplication with
blocking optimization

void matrix_multiply_blocked(const
std::vector<std::vector<double>>& A, const
std::vector<std::vector<double>>& B,
std::vector<std::vector<double>>& C, int block_size) {

    int n = A.size();

    for (int i = 0; i < n; i += block_size) {

        for (int j = 0; j < n; j += block_size) {

            for (int k = 0; k < n; k += block_size) {

                // Perform matrix multiplication for the
current block

                for (int ii = i; ii < std::min(i +
block_size, n); ++ii) {

                    for (int jj = j; jj < std::min(j +
block_size, n); ++jj) {

                        for (int kk = k; kk < std::min(k
+ block_size, n); ++kk) {
```

```
                            C[ii][jj] += A[ii][kk] *
B[kk][jj];
                        }
                    }
                }
            }
        }
    }
}

int main() {
    // Initialize two 3x3 matrices
    std::vector<std::vector<double>> A = {
        {1.0, 2.0, 3.0},
        {4.0, 5.0, 6.0},
        {7.0, 8.0, 9.0}
    };
    std::vector<std::vector<double>> B = {
        {9.0, 8.0, 7.0},
        {6.0, 5.0, 4.0},
        {3.0, 2.0, 1.0}
    };
```

```
    std::vector<std::vector<double>> C(3,
std::vector<double>(3));

    int block_size = 2;  // Set block size for blocking
optimization

    // Perform matrix multiplication with blocking
    matrix_multiply_blocked(A, B, C, block_size);

    // Output the result
    std::cout << "Resulting matrix with blocking
optimization:\n";
    for (const auto& row : C) {
        for (double val : row) {
            std::cout << val << " ";
        }
        std::cout << "\n";
    }

    return 0;
}
```

In the above, instead of processing each element individually, the matrix is divided into smaller blocks of size **block_size**. By processing the blocks, we improve the usage of the CPU cache, as blocks are loaded into the cache and reused before being evicted. The smaller blocks fit into the CPU cache, reducing the number of cache misses and improving memory access speeds. The blocking implementation uses three outer loops to iterate over the blocks of matrices **A**, **B**, and **C**, and three inner loops to perform the actual matrix multiplication for each block.

By using this optimization, we can achieve better performance, especially for large matrices. The exact performance gain depends on the size of the matrices and the block size chosen, but in general, blocking leads to significant improvements in cache utilization and processing speed.

Optimizing Trigonometric Operations

In real-time physics simulations, trigonometric functions like sine, cosine, and tangent are often used in rotation and transformation calculations. While the standard library implementations of these functions are accurate, they may not be fast enough for real-time applications that require thousands or millions of such calculations per second.

One way to speed up trigonometric calculations is to use **precomputed lookup tables**. By precomputing the values of sine and cosine for a range of angles, we can reduce the time required to perform these calculations during runtime. Following is how we can implement a lookup table for sine and cosine:

```
#include <iostream>

#include <vector>

#include <cmath>

// Function to generate lookup tables for sine and cosine

void generate_trig_tables(std::vector<double>& sin_table,
std::vector<double>& cos_table, int num_angles) {

    for (int i = 0; i < num_angles; ++i) {

        double angle = (i * 2 * M_PI) / num_angles;  //
Convert index to angle in radians

        sin_table[i] = std::sin(angle);

        cos_table[i] = std::cos(angle);

    }
```

```
}

// Function to use the precomputed lookup table for sine
double fast_sin(const std::vector<double>& sin_table, int
index) {
    return sin_table[index];
}

// Function to use the precomputed lookup table for
cosine
double fast_cos(const std::vector<double>& cos_table, int
index) {
    return cos_table[index];
}

int main() {
    int num_angles = 360;  // Number of angles to
precompute (1-degree resolution)
    std::vector<double> sin_table(num_angles);
    std::vector<double> cos_table(num_angles);

    // Generate the sine and cosine lookup tables
```

```
    generate_trig_tables(sin_table, cos_table,
num_angles);


    // Use the precomputed values for fast sine and
cosine calculations

    int angle_index = 90;  // Example: 90 degrees (index
90)

    std::cout << "Fast sine of 90 degrees: " <<
fast_sin(sin_table, angle_index) << "\n";

    std::cout << "Fast cosine of 90 degrees: " <<
fast_cos(cos_table, angle_index) << "\n";


    return 0;

}
```

Here,

- we precompute the sine and cosine values for a range of angles (in this case, 0 to 360 degrees) and store them in lookup tables. This allows us to retrieve the values instantly during runtime, eliminating the need to calculate the sine and cosine functions repeatedly.
- And, instead of calling **std::sin()** and **std::cos()** during the simulation, we simply look up the precomputed values in the tables, significantly speeding up the calculation.

By using techniques like blocking and lookup tables, we can significantly speed up these operations, enabling real-time performance in computationally demanding applications. These optimizations ensure that our mathematical operations are both fast and accurate, meeting the needs of high-performance computing tasks.

Take Control with Fixed-Point Arithmetic

Basics of Fixed-Point Arithmetic

Fixed-point arithmetic offers a powerful alternative to floating-point arithmetic, particularly in performance-critical applications where precise control over number representation is needed. Unlike floating-point numbers, which provide dynamic ranges but can introduce rounding errors, fixed-point numbers represent values with a fixed number of digits before and after the decimal point. This allows for greater precision and predictability, especially in systems where hardware or performance constraints make floating-point operations too slow or imprecise.

Fixed-point arithmetic is particularly valuable in **embedded systems**, **real-time applications**, and **digital signal processing (DSP)**, where the deterministic behavior and reduced computational overhead are critical. In such systems, the precision requirements are known in advance, and the lack of floating-point units (FPUs) in many embedded processors makes floating-point operations expensive in terms of both time and energy consumption.

Fixed-point numbers are represented with a fixed number of bits allocated to the integer part and the fractional part. For example, a fixed-point number with 16 bits might allocate 8 bits to the integer part and 8 bits to the fractional part, effectively allowing us to represent numbers in the range of −128.0-128.0−128.0 to 127.99609375127.99609375127.99609375 with a precision of 1/2561/2561/256. This fixed allocation simplifies arithmetic operations like addition, subtraction, and multiplication, as the operations can be performed using integer arithmetic, which is faster and more predictable than floating-point arithmetic.

Performance Benefits of Fixed-Point Arithmetic

Fixed-point arithmetic provides several advantages over floating-point arithmetic, particularly in performance-critical applications like embedded systems and real-time control systems:

- **Speed**: Fixed-point arithmetic is typically faster than floating-point arithmetic, especially on hardware without floating-point units (FPUs). Many embedded processors lack FPUs, meaning that floating-point operations must be emulated in software, which is significantly slower than integer arithmetic.
- **Predictability**: In real-time systems, predictable execution times are essential. Fixed-point arithmetic has deterministic performance, meaning that the time taken to perform operations is constant, unlike floating-point arithmetic, where performance can vary depending on the values being processed.
- **Memory Efficiency**: Fixed-point numbers use fewer bits to represent the same range of values as floating-point numbers. This is particularly important in systems with limited memory, such as microcontrollers.
- **Precision Control**: With fixed-point arithmetic, we can explicitly control the precision by adjusting the number of bits allocated to the fractional part. This allows us to fine-tune the trade-off between precision and range to suit the needs of the application.

Implementing Fixed-Point Arithmetic

We will create a simple class to represent fixed-point numbers and demonstrate how to perform arithmetic operations with them. In our case, we will use 16 bits to represent the numbers, with 8 bits for the integer part and 8 bits for the fractional part.

```
#include <iostream>

#include <cstdint>


class FixedPoint {

public:

    FixedPoint(int32_t value = 0) : raw_value(value) {}


    // Conversion from double to fixed-point

    FixedPoint(double value) {

        raw_value = static_cast<int32_t>(value *
scaling_factor);

    }


    // Conversion to double for output

    double to_double() const {

        return static_cast<double>(raw_value) /
scaling_factor;

    }
```

```
    // Addition
    FixedPoint operator+(const FixedPoint& other) const {
        return FixedPoint(raw_value + other.raw_value);
    }

    // Subtraction
    FixedPoint operator-(const FixedPoint& other) const {
        return FixedPoint(raw_value - other.raw_value);
    }

    // Multiplication
    FixedPoint operator*(const FixedPoint& other) const {
        // Multiplying two fixed-point numbers requires
scaling adjustment
        return FixedPoint((raw_value * other.raw_value) /
scaling_factor);
    }

    // Division
    FixedPoint operator/(const FixedPoint& other) const {
        // Division requires scaling adjustment to
maintain precision
```

```
        return FixedPoint((raw_value * scaling_factor) /
other.raw_value);
    }

    // Output the value
    void print() const {
        std::cout << to_double() << std::endl;
    }

private:
    int32_t raw_value;  // Stores the fixed-point value
as an integer
    static constexpr int32_t scaling_factor = 256;  // 8
fractional bits (2^8 = 256)
};

int main() {
    // Initialize fixed-point numbers representing
temperatures
    FixedPoint temp1(22.75);  // 22.75 degrees Celsius
    FixedPoint temp2(18.5);   // 18.5 degrees Celsius

    // Perform arithmetic operations
```

```
    FixedPoint sum = temp1 + temp2;

    FixedPoint diff = temp1 - temp2;

    FixedPoint product = temp1 * FixedPoint(2.0);  //
Multiply by 2 (scaling adjustment handled automatically)

    FixedPoint quotient = temp1 / FixedPoint(1.5);  //
Divide by 1.5


    // Output the results

    std::cout << "Sum: "; sum.print();

    std::cout << "Difference: "; diff.print();

    std::cout << "Product: "; product.print();

    std::cout << "Quotient: "; quotient.print();


    return 0;

}
```

Here, the **FixedPoint** class stores the number as an integer (**raw_value**), representing both the integer and fractional parts. A scaling factor of 256 is used, corresponding to 8 fractional bits. This allows us to represent fractional numbers with a precision of 1/2561/2561/256. The constructor allows us to initialize a fixed-point number from a **double**. The value is multiplied by the scaling factor and then cast to an integer, storing it as a fixed-point value.

In the **main()** function, we represent two temperature readings (**22.75** and **18.5** degrees Celsius) using fixed-point arithmetic. We perform basic arithmetic operations (addition, subtraction, multiplication, and division) and output the results.

Sample Program: Fixed-Point Arithmetic for Temperature Control

We will extend our previous temperature control system to simulate a real-time feedback loop where the system adjusts a heating element based on the difference between the current temperature and the desired setpoint. This simulation requires fast, precise calculations, making fixed-point arithmetic an ideal choice.

```
#include <iostream>

#include <cstdint>


class FixedPoint {

public:

    FixedPoint(int32_t value = 0) : raw_value(value) {}


    FixedPoint(double value) {

        raw_value = static_cast<int32_t>(value *
scaling_factor);

    }


    double to_double() const {

        return static_cast<double>(raw_value) /
scaling_factor;

    }


    FixedPoint operator+(const FixedPoint& other) const {

        return FixedPoint(raw_value + other.raw_value);

    }
```

```
    FixedPoint operator-(const FixedPoint& other) const {

        return FixedPoint(raw_value - other.raw_value);

    }


    void print() const {

        std::cout << to_double() << std::endl;

    }


private:

    int32_t raw_value;

    static constexpr int32_t scaling_factor = 256;

};


void control_temperature(const FixedPoint& current_temp,
const FixedPoint& target_temp) {

    FixedPoint error = target_temp - current_temp;

    FixedPoint adjustment = error * FixedPoint(0.1);  //
Adjust temperature based on error


    std::cout << "Adjustment needed: ";
adjustment.print();
```

```
}


int main() {
    FixedPoint current_temp(21.5);   // Current
temperature in degrees Celsius
    FixedPoint target_temp(23.0);    // Target temperature
in degrees Celsius


    control_temperature(current_temp, target_temp);


    return 0;
}
```

In the above sample script, we simulate a simple feedback loop where the difference between the current and target temperatures is calculated using fixed-point arithmetic, and the heating element is adjusted accordingly. The use of fixed-point arithmetic ensures that the calculations are both fast and precise, making it ideal for real-time control systems in embedded devices.

Master Mathematical Constants and Rounding

In C++23, handling mathematical constants and rounding operations has been significantly improved, allowing developers to write more accurate and efficient code. Mathematical constants like π (pi), e (Euler's number), and others have been introduced as part of the standard library, simplifying access to these commonly used values without relying on custom definitions or external libraries. Additionally, the improvements in rounding techniques give developers finer control over how values are rounded, ensuring that numerical precision is maintained in performance-critical applications.

In this section, we will revisit one of our previously demonstrated programs, the temperature control system using fixed-point arithmetic, and show how the introduction of new mathematical constants and rounding techniques in C++23 can enhance numeric calculations.

Mathematical Constants

Prior to C++23, developers had to manually define commonly used mathematical constants or rely on external libraries. Now, C++23 introduces standardized constants that can be used directly from the **std::numbers** namespace, ensuring consistent precision across different compilers and platforms.

Some of the important constants introduced include:

- π (**std::numbers::pi**): Represents the mathematical constant pi, approximately equal to 3.141592653589793.
- e (**std::numbers::e**): Represents Euler's number, approximately equal to 2.718281828459045.
- Golden ratio (**std::numbers::phi**): Represents the golden ratio, approximately equal to 1.618033988749895.

These constants can be directly used in calculations without the need to define them manually, ensuring that the precision provided by the constants is consistent and optimized for the platform.

Applying Mathematical Constants in a Temperature Control System

We will consider our temperature control system, where the current and target temperatures are adjusted based on a feedback loop. In a real-world system, you might need to apply some transformation to the temperature values, such as scaling the adjustments by a factor of π to reflect the geometry of the system (for example, adjusting the temperature in a circular heating system).

Here, we will demonstrate how to integrate these mathematical constants into the system.

```
#include <iostream>

#include <cstdint>

#include <numbers>  // For mathematical constants



class FixedPoint {

public:

    FixedPoint(int32_t value = 0) : raw_value(value) {}
```

```
    FixedPoint(double value) {
        raw_value = static_cast<int32_t>(value *
scaling_factor);
    }

    double to_double() const {
        return static_cast<double>(raw_value) /
scaling_factor;
    }

    FixedPoint operator+(const FixedPoint& other) const {
        return FixedPoint(raw_value + other.raw_value);
    }

    FixedPoint operator-(const FixedPoint& other) const {
        return FixedPoint(raw_value - other.raw_value);
    }

    FixedPoint operator*(const FixedPoint& other) const {
        return FixedPoint((raw_value * other.raw_value) /
scaling_factor);
```

```
    }

    void print() const {
        std::cout << to_double() << std::endl;
    }

private:
    int32_t raw_value;
    static constexpr int32_t scaling_factor = 256;  // Scaling factor for fixed-point representation
};

// Function to control the temperature, applying a constant factor (e.g., pi) for scaling
void control_temperature_with_pi(const FixedPoint& current_temp, const FixedPoint& target_temp) {
    FixedPoint error = target_temp - current_temp;

    // Scale the adjustment by pi (for example, to reflect the circular nature of the system)
    FixedPoint pi_factor(std::numbers::pi);
    FixedPoint adjustment = error * pi_factor;
```

```
    std::cout << "Adjustment needed (scaled by pi): ";
    adjustment.print();
}

int main() {
    FixedPoint current_temp(21.5);  // Current
temperature in degrees Celsius
    FixedPoint target_temp(23.0);   // Target temperature
in degrees Celsius
    control_temperature_with_pi(current_temp,
target_temp);

    return 0;
}
```

Here, we use the mathematical constant π (**std::numbers::pi**) to scale the adjustment needed for the temperature control system. This demonstrates how constants from the **std::numbers** namespace can be seamlessly integrated into existing programs. By doing this, we avoid the potential pitfalls of manually defining the constant and ensure maximum precision.

In the **control_temperature_with_pi()** function, the adjustment to the temperature is scaled by the value of π. This could represent a real-world scenario, such as adjusting the temperature around a circular heating element, where the geometry of the system requires the adjustment to be scaled by a factor related to π.

By using predefined mathematical constants, we ensure that the precision is maintained throughout the calculation. The **std::numbers** constants are optimized for performance and precision, ensuring that rounding errors and truncations are minimized.

Improved Rounding Techniques

In C++23, several new rounding modes have been introduced that give developers finer control over how rounding is handled. These rounding modes are essential in applications like financial systems, scientific computing, and embedded systems, where even small rounding errors can lead to significant deviations over time.

Some of the new rounding techniques introduced in C++23 include:

- **std::midpoint()**: Computes the exact midpoint of two numbers, preventing overflow.
- **std::lerp()**: Performs linear interpolation between two values, rounding the result to the nearest representable value.
- **std::round()**, **std::floor()**, **std::ceil()**: These functions have been improved to handle edge cases more effectively and provide more predictable rounding behavior.

We will demonstrate how these improved rounding techniques can be applied to optimize numeric calculations in our temperature control system.

Applying Improved Rounding Techniques

In our temperature control system, suppose we want to ensure that temperature adjustments are always rounded to the nearest 0.1 degree for display purposes. This requires precise control over how the values are rounded, ensuring that the displayed value is both accurate and easy to read.

We will use **std::round()** to round the temperature values to the nearest 0.1 degree and demonstrate how rounding can be optimized for performance and precision.

```
#include <iostream>

#include <cmath>    // For rounding functions


class FixedPoint {

public:

    FixedPoint(int32_t value = 0) : raw_value(value) {}



    FixedPoint(double value) {
```

```
        raw_value = static_cast<int32_t>(value *
scaling_factor);
    }

    double to_double() const {
        return static_cast<double>(raw_value) /
scaling_factor;
    }

    FixedPoint operator+(const FixedPoint& other) const {
        return FixedPoint(raw_value + other.raw_value);
    }

    FixedPoint operator-(const FixedPoint& other) const {
        return FixedPoint(raw_value - other.raw_value);
    }

    void print() const {
        std::cout << std::round(to_double() * 10) / 10 <<
std::endl;  // Rounding to nearest 0.1 degree
    }
```

```
private:
    int32_t raw_value;
    static constexpr int32_t scaling_factor = 256;  //
Scaling factor for fixed-point representation
};


int main() {
    FixedPoint current_temp(21.57);  // Current
temperature in degrees Celsius
    FixedPoint target_temp(23.06);   // Target
temperature in degrees Celsius

    std::cout << "Current temperature (rounded to nearest
0.1): ";
    current_temp.print();

    std::cout << "Target temperature (rounded to nearest
0.1): ";
    target_temp.print();

    return 0;
}
```

In the **print()** function, we use **std::round()** to round the temperature value to the nearest 0.1 degree. This is done by multiplying the value by 10, rounding it to the nearest integer, and then dividing by 10 to get the final result.

By rounding the temperature values to the nearest 0.1 degree, we ensure that the system displays user-friendly values while maintaining the precision required for the control system's calculations. This is particularly important in systems where small rounding errors can lead to instability or incorrect results.

By combining the new mathematical constants and improved rounding techniques, we can optimize numeric calculations in performance-critical applications like embedded systems, real-time simulations, and scientific computing. The use of standardized constants ensures consistent precision across platforms, while the new rounding modes give developers finer control over how values are truncated or rounded, reducing the risk of cumulative errors.

Summary

Ultimately, the goal was to enhance numerical computations by exploring methods to more precisely and efficiently manage integer and floating-point operations. The chapter began with arbitrary precision arithmetic, which overcame the limitations of standard floating-point types using libraries like GMP. Following that, we focused on optimizing arithmetic operations with efficient algorithms. We looked at matrix multiplication and trigonometric operations, demonstrating how techniques like blocking and lookup tables can significantly improve performance.

The emphasis then shifted to fixed-point arithmetic, which proved useful in performance-critical applications, particularly embedded and real-time systems. The chapter ended with the introduction of new mathematical constants and improved rounding methods. We simplified complex calculations and ensured precision consistency by using standard library constants such as π and Euler's number. Furthermore, advanced rounding techniques enabled more accurate truncation and rounding, reducing errors in numeric calculations. These enhancements assembled a complete set of tools for optimizing numerical operations in modern C++ scripting.

Index

A

Arbitrary precision arithmetic 242
Async IO 100
Atomic operations 223

B

Blocking 62, 250
Buffering 100, 101, 102, 107

C

Cache-aware programming 165
Callables 49
Condition variables 196
Custom allocators 158, 159

D

Deadlock 190, 192, 221
Deadlock detection 221
Direct file manipulation 71
Direct IO 117

E

Event-driven programming 108

F

File descriptors 60, 68
Fixed-point arithmetic 257
Fold expressions 7, 8, 9, 10
Function overloading 39
Futures 228, 229, 233, 235

G

Golden ratio 265

L

Load balancing 205
Lock-free data structures 235, 239

M

Mathematical constants 264
Matrix multiplication 248
Memory alignment 136, 172
Mutexes 188, 190

P

Parameter packs 3, 4, 20, 21, 25
Perfect forwarding 4, 22, 23, 47
Priority inheritance 223
Promises 228, 229, 233

R

Recursion 7

S

SIMD instructions 250
Smart pointers 148

T

Task synchronization 205
Template metaprogramming 32

V

Variadic templates 2, 3, 5

Epilogue

I am pleased to say that by the time this book comes to a close, we have covered most of the material in C++23's advanced topics. When I set out to write "Modern C++23 QuickStart Pro," my goal was to make sure that developers could make the most of the language's newest features. My goal was to never overwhelm you. I want you to see C++ in a new light—one in which the complexity is no longer a burden, but rather a tool you can use with precision. Especially when confronted with an ever-expanding set of features and possibilities, modern C++ can feel overwhelming, as I know from personal experience. But you can overcome it. The complexities of variadic templates and lock-free data structures can be overwhelming.

With the knowledge you gained in these chapters, you will be able to optimize low-level I/O, construct scalable multi-threaded systems, and master advanced function signatures. By now, you should be able to manage memory, create custom allocators, and understand cache behavior like a pro. We have become experts in numerical operations, guaranteeing accuracy when it matters most, and in thread synchronization without compromising speed. Having these abilities will not leave you feeling helpless; on the contrary, they will provide you with real-world tools that can alleviate a lot of stress. You've tackled concepts that were previously difficult to grasp, and you now have a better understanding and command of the language.

It's been a long road, but one worth taking. You are now prepared to take advantage of C++23's vast potential. Whether you're optimizing a high-performance application, developing robust multi-threaded systems, or pushing the limits of numerical precision, you're prepared to face any challenge. You are now on solid ground, prepared to face the complex and exciting world of C++23 with confidence. Although there is always more to discover, I hope that this book has provided you with the necessary tools and inspiration to keep moving ahead. For now, however, take a moment to reflect on how far you've come.

Well done! You've successfully learned this book.

Thank You

www.ingramcontent.com/pod-product-compliance
Lightning Source LLC
Chambersburg PA
CBHW080210170726
48282CB00030B/1061
* 9 7 8 8 1 9 7 4 1 6 5 6 9 *